TWAYNE'S WORLD AUTHORS SERIES

A Survey of the World's Literature

Sylvia E. Bowman, Indiana University

GENERAL EDITOR

GERMANY

Ulrich Weisstein, Indiana University

EDITOR

Friedrich Schlegel

(*TWAS 98*)

TWAYNE'S WORLD AUTHORS SERIES (TWAS)

The purpose of TWAS is to survey the major writers —novelists, dramatists, historians, poets, philosophers, and critics—of the nations of the world. Among the national literatures covered are those of Australia, Canada, China, Eastern Europe, France, Germany, Greece, India, Italy, Japan, Latin America, New Zealand, Poland, Russia, Scandinavia, Spain, and the African nations, as well as Hebrew, Yiddish, and Latin Classical literatures. This survey is complemented by Twayne's United States Authors Series and English Authors Series.

The intent of each volume in these series is to present a critical-analytical study of the works of the writer; to include biographical and historical material that may be necessary for understanding, appreciation, and critical appraisal of the writer; and to present all material in clear, concise English—but not to vitiate the scholarly content of the work by doing so.

Friedrich Schlegel

By HANS EICHNER
University of Toronto

Twayne Publishers, Inc.　::　New York

Preface

LITERARY critic and theorist, poet and novelist, classical phi-
lologist and Sanskrit scholar, philosopher and theologian,
innovator in the appreciation of painting and architecture, Friedrich Schlegel was active in more fields than any biographer is
likely to be competent in. To do full justice to him in any single
work would be difficult; to do so in a very short work is impossible. The present book is thus offered to the reader merely as an
introduction, with the awareness that there are many aspects of
Schlegel's life and works that are barely touched upon, and none
that could be treated in full; but it is also offered in the conviction
that such an introduction is badly needed: at the moment of
writing, no full-length "life and works" of Friedrich Schlegel exists
in any language.[1]

In view of Schlegel's importance in the history of literature, I
hope that this book will find readers also among those who read
little or no German; quotations, therefore, are given throughout
in English translation. The German original is provided in the
notes to the limited extent to which the available space permitted
this practice, preference being given to passages that do not lend
themselves to literal translation, passages that seemed particularly
important, and (though this rule was not followed consistently)
to short rather than long quotations. Titles are given in the original
German, since any other practice would have led to confusion
and ambiguities. Translations are provided in the index.

My research on Friedrich Schlegel—both for the present book
and for the critical edition of Schlegel's works—has been supported most generously by the Canada Council, the Heinrich
Hertz Foundation, the Nuffield Foundation, and Queen's University. Most of the book was written in the leisure time provided
for me by a McLaughlin Research Professorship at the last-named
of these institutions, to all of which I am profoundly indebted.

41611

Last but not least, I should like to thank my friends and colleagues, Professors Ernst Behler, Martyn Estall, K. K. Polheim, and A. W. Riley for help, advice, and encouragement throughout many years.

H. E.

Toronto,
April 30, 1968.

Contents

Chronology

1767 August Wilhelm Schlegel born on September 8 in Hanover.
1772 Friedrich Schlegel born on March 9 in Hanover.
1790 Friedrich commences his studies in Göttingen.
1791 He moves to Leipzig (May).
1792 Beginning of his friendship with Novalis.
1793 He meets Caroline.
1794 Move to Dresden (January). Publication of his earliest essays on the Greeks (October–December).
1795 Completion of the essay "Über das Studium der griechischen Poesie" (December).
1796 Schlegel begins to publish reviews in Reichardt's *Deutschland*. He moves to Jena (August).
1797 Schlegel's first book—*Die Griechen und Römer*, containing the essay "Über das Studium der griechischen Poesie"—published in January. Publication of the essays "Georg Forster" and "Über Lessing," and of the "Lyceums–Fragmente." In July, Schlegel moves to Berlin, where he meets Tieck, Schleiermacher, and Dorothea Veit.
1798 Founding of the *Athenäum*. *Geschichte der Poesie der Griechen und Römer*. "Athenäums-Fragmente." "Über Goethes Meister."
1799 *Lucinde*. Schlegel returns to Jena (September).
1800 "Ideen." "Gespräch über die Poesie." Discontinuation of the *Athenäum*. Schlegel lectures on transcendental philosophy (October 27–March 24, 1801). He begins to write poetry.
1801 Novalis dies. Friedrich quarrels with his brother. In December, he leaves Jena and visits Berlin.
1802 *Alarcos* published and performed. Schlegel visits Dresden (January–May), then settles in Paris. He begins to write on painting and to study Sanskrit.

1803 *Europa* (first three issues). Schlegel lectures to the brothers Boisserée on literature and philosophy.

1804 *Lessings Gedanken und Meinungen.* In April, Schlegel marries Dorothea and moves to Cologne, where he lectures extensively on philosophy. He visits Mme de Staël in Coppet (October–November), then returns to Paris to continue his Sanskrit studies.

1805 Schlegel returns to Cologne (March). He lectures on history, but fails to secure suitable employment. *Europa* (4th and final issue). *Poetisches Taschenbuch für das Jahr 1806* (containing Schlegel's letters on Gothic architecture and many poems).

1806 Schlegel visits Mme de Staël in Aubergenville, where he stays as her guest from November to April, 1807.

1807 Schlegel lectures to the brothers Boisserée on German language and literature.

1808 *Über die Sprache und Weisheit der Indier.* Reviews in the *Heidelbergische Jahrbücher.* Formal act of conversion to Roman Catholicism (April 16). Move to Vienna.

1809 Schlegel enters the Austrian civil service (March); he edits the *Österreichische Zeitung* (June–December).

1810 Schlegel delivers his lectures *Über die neuere Geschichte* (published 1811) and edits the *Österreichischer Beobachter.*

1812 He delivers his lectures on ancient and modern literature (published 1815) and edits the *Deutsches Museum* (1812–13).

1815 He is appointed to the Austrian Legation at the Diet of Frankfort (October).

1818 Dorothea visits her sons in Italy, where she stays till 1820. Schlegel returns to Vienna (November).

1819 Schlegel visits Italy. He begins to publish essays on theology.

1820 He edits the periodical *Concordia.*

1821 Schlegel begins to exchange letters with Christine von Stransky.

1822–1825 His *Sämtliche Werke* are published in ten volumes.

1827 Schlegel lectures on *Philosophie des Lebens* (published 1828).

Chronology

1828   He lectures on *Philosophie der Geschichte* (published 1829). In December, he goes to Dresden to lecture on *Philosophie der Sprache* (published 1830).

1829   Schlegel dies in Dresden in the early hours of January 12.

CHAPTER 1

The Beginnings

FRIEDRICH Schlegel—or, to give his full name, Carl Friedrich August Schlegel—was born in Hanover on March 10, 1772, as the scion of a family illustrious in German literature. His uncle, Johann Elias Schlegel (1718–49), had been a successful dramatist and ranks as Lessing's most brilliant forerunner in the field of esthetics. His father, Johann Adolf Schlegel (1721–93), had been the co-founder of an important literary group, the *Bremer Beiträger,* and had produced an influential, profusely annotated translation of Batteux' *Les Beaux-Arts réduits à un même principe.* A clergyman by profession, he became, in 1775, the *pastor primarius* of a large church, the Neustadt *Hof- und Stadtkirche.* There were five sons. The two eldest, Karl August Moriz (1756–1826) and Johann Karl Fürchtegott (1758–1831), both entered the Church. Characteristically, they both wrote books, mainly on theological subjects. The third, Karl August (1761–89), became an army officer and died in the service of the East India Company. The fourth, August Wilhelm Schlegel (1767–1845), is the critic and poet whose fame, for almost a century, overshadowed that of his younger brother, and whose translations of Shakespeare are still unsurpassed.

By the time Friedrich, the youngest of the five brothers, was born, his uncle had long been dead; and his father was never very close to him. The break between the two generations is illustrated by the fact that neither Johann Elias nor Johann Adolf Schlegel were ever mentioned in the histories of literature Friedrich wrote; but his position as an heir to a rich literary tradition and as a "latecomer" is nevertheless significant: if there is anything that the leading members of the young, Romantic[1] generation indubitably had in common, it was their passion for books and the accompanying tendency to look at the world through the colored glasses of literature.

We know very little about Friedrich's childhood. A difficult and ailing child, he was first farmed out to an uncle, then to his brother Moriz. Upon his return to Hanover, his education was largely left in the hands of August Wilhelm, who was himself still a schoolboy; and at the age of fifteen he was apprenticed to a banker in Leipzig, where he was desperately unhappy. Less than two years later, he was permitted to return home and instructed to learn enough Latin and Greek to be admitted to a university. A local schoolmaster was called in for help, and now Friedrich, sullen and undecided until this moment, found his first spiritual home. By the time he was eighteen, he had mastered both classical languages and had read the Greek dramatists and the whole of Plato in the original. A visit to Dresden, where he spent hours of enchantment among Mengs' plastercasts of classical statues, completed the process: the student who, in 1790, moved to the University of Göttingen, was a confirmed admirer of classical antiquity.

At Göttingen, where he spent less than a year, and at Leipzig, where he lived from May, 1791, to January, 1794, Schlegel was supposed to study Law, but did not pay very much attention to this subject. However, he did not waste his time—or at least not at first. He already knew French and Spanish and now improved his command of English and Italian. He read unsystematically but encyclopedically, gaining some knowledge of mathematics and the natural sciences, and an extensive knowledge of philosophy, history, and literature. His intellectual curiosity was insatiable, and he read at a speed and with a power of concentration that amazed his acquaintances. It is scarcely surprising that he was aware of his own brilliance, but this realization brought him no happiness. His letters from Leipzig are a vivid testimony of his restlessness, of his dissatisfaction with a mode of life that failed to satisfy what he called, with a characteristic phrase, his "thirst for the infinite," and, above all, of his dissatisfaction with himself.

Compulsive introspection—the state of mind in which a person cannot do or say anything without, at the same time, watching himself do or say it—is a frequent phenomenon with gifted adolescents. Schlegel could not shake this habit until he was well in his twenties, and his introspection invariably led him to the same conclusion—that his intellect was dissociated from the rest of his personality and dominated it to an extent that threatened to destroy him. "I love nothing, nobody," he wrote to his brother Wilhelm in October, 1791. "Consider what these words mean and count yourself fortunate in that you have great sorrows."—"I am intelligent," he complained two years later, "but I am so inexperienced, so limited and, above all—it would be unjust to deny that I have a soul, but quite obviously I lack the soul's soul [*die Seele der Seele*], the capacity to love." "I know that I cannot live unless I achieve greatness—i.e., self-satisfaction. For my intelligence is such that if my other faculties were equal to it and in harmony, I would already have achieved greatness." [2]

Driven by his fear of emotional atrophy, Friedrich attempted a cure. He cold-bloodedly went in search of someone to fall in love with, rather foolishly chose a married woman who moved in circles which the young student could ill afford to join, and in short order succeeded in talking himself into a state of frenzied passion. The object of his love, whom he attempted to conquer by elaborate schemes that smack of cheap novelettes, toyed with him for a while and then dropped him. Friedrich now strove to drown his sorrows—the hackneyed phrase seems appropriate—in what he rather vaguely called "debauches" and "excesses," [3] mainly, it appears, at the gambling table. He lost heavily, borrowed money where he could, paid old debts by contracting new ones at exorbitant rates of interest, and by the fall of 1793 faced financial ruin. In the nick of time, his brother Wilhelm came to the rescue, parting with most of his savings to avoid a catastrophe; but by the end of 1794 Friedrich's debts still amounted to several times his annual income, and he was pursued by creditors to the end of his life.

In the two-and-a-half years he spent in Leipzig, he was repeatedly on the verge of committing suicide. From the end of spring, 1793, however, the turbulence of his letters to his brother—our main source of information on this stage in Friedrich's life—began to abate. In July of the same year, he made the acquaintance of his future sister-in-law, Caroline Böhmer, and a relationship developed between the two that greatly accelerated Friedrich's recovery. The daughter of the orientalist Michaelis at Göttingen, Caroline had, at the age of twenty, married a country doctor, who had died within four years of the marriage. After a stay at Göttingen, where A. W. Schlegel met her and fell in love with her, she had moved to Mainz, which, in October, 1792, was occupied by the French. There, she lived at the house of Georg Forster, who belonged to the pro-revolutionary clubbists at Mainz, and whose views she shared. In the winter of that year, she had a fleeting love affair with a young French officer, and when, in the following spring, she tried to escape from Mainz, which was by then surrounded by Prussian troops, she was caught, imprisoned as a revolutionary in Fort Königstein, and now, in the most desperate situation, found that she was pregnant. Her brother secured her release, and Wilhelm found her a hiding place in the town of Lucka, three miles from Leipzig, where she was safe from political persecution and could await her confinement in secrecy. As Wilhelm had to return to his job as a tutor in Amsterdam, her care was entrusted to Friedrich.

In later years, Friedrich occasionally hinted that he had been in love with Caroline during her stay in Lucka; all we can be sure of is that he greatly admired her. For the first time in his life he had found a woman who understood him and whose intelligence was equal to his own. Her brilliant insight into contemporary German poetry stimulated his interests; her courage in adversity shamed him into fighting his fits of depression; her sympathy, advice, and friendly mockery helped him to gain control of himself and to face his problems in a more practical manner. Last but not least, she instilled in him a fervent desire to earn her respect and admiration, and so, after three years of erratic reading and time-wasting, he began to work toward a specific end.

A few weeks before Caroline arrived in Lucka, Friedrich had decided to give up his legal studies. "I realize the obvious impossibility," he had written to his brother in June, 1793, "of submitting to the yoke of a bourgeois profession . . . My aim is . . . to live, to live in freedom . . . You have known me for such a long time; think about me once again and tell me what I am destined for, what is to become of me, what I am to do!" [4] By the fall of the same year, he appears to have decided to make a living as a free-lance writer. In November, he had started to work on three essays on Greek literature, to this end reread the great Athenian dramatists, and now fell under their spell even more completely than he had done five years previously. By February, 1794, having, in the meantime, stolen away from Leipzig and his creditors and settled in Dresden, he had decided on the great project that was to remain, for the next two years, his work during the day and his dream at night: a monumental history of classical poetry.

Schlegel now radically changed his way of life. He avoided company, rose at dawn, and worked till late into the night. But the project he had undertaken was vast, and in spite of prodigious efforts, the first and, as it turned out, only volume of his *Geschichte der Poesie der Griechen und Römer* was not completed until 1798, by which time his views had undergone a considerable change. In his first two years at Dresden, however, he wrote some preliminary studies towards the *Geschichte* that reveal very clearly the kind of fascination the Greeks had for him: five articles published in 1794 and 1795 in various periodicals; an essay with the title "Vom Wert des Studiums der Griechen und Römer," [5] which remained unpublished during his lifetime; and a much more extensive second treatment of this subject, completed in 1795 and published in January, 1797, with the title "Über das Studium der griechischen Poesie." [6]

The views Schlegel presented in these essays are not strikingly original; in the main, they consisted in an ingenious systematization of an attitude toward ancient and modern literature that was very wide-spread in German literary circles toward the end of the eighteenth century. This attitude had first been propagated with brilliant persuasiveness by J. J. Winckelmann (1717–68) in his *Gedanken über die Nachahmung der griechischen Werke in der Malerei und Bildhauerkunst* (1755) and in his monumental *Geschichte der Kunst des Altertums* (1764). Since then, Winckelmann's ideas had gained an increasing number of adherents, and in the first half of the 1790's, views similar to his were advanced by Goethe and Schiller, as well as by a host of minor writers such as Heydenreich, Garve, and Bouterwek.[7] Schlegel read them all, and both his own theories and the terminology in which he presented them show the influence of Goethe, Schiller and Kant. Even so, the decisive impression had been made on him by Winckelmann himself, whom he had first read in Hanover as a teen-ager and reread repeatedly since, and who remained the only person to whom Schlegel ever referred to as his "master." [8] Of course, Winckelmann was concerned with sculpture rather than with poetry, but this by no means lessens his importance; on the contrary, the history of German poetics in the second half of the eighteenth century can only be fully understood if it is realized to what extent current utterances about poetry were indebted to views originally abstracted from a study of the visual arts.

Nature, Winckelmann held, had provided the Greeks with an ideal environment, which, combined with a healthy way of life, endowed them with exceptional physical beauty. Thus, Greek artists had better models than their modern counterparts, and as they were not inhibited by Christian notions of modesty, they could study these models under better conditions. Even so, they were not content with the mere copying of the splendid subjects with which Nature so generously supplied them. While the artists of other nations, according to Winckelmann, aimed at such things as the extraordinary, like the ancient Egyptians, or at originality and the realism of portraiture, like many moderns, the Greek artists aspired single-mindedly to one supreme goal—perfect beauty. Now, Winckelmann argued, no natural thing is ever perfectly beautiful. Realizing this, the Greeks were not satisfied with the "individual beauty" to be found even in the best models, but strove to surpass nature by a process of idealization. The wise artists of antiquity, Winckelmann taught,

proceeded like a clever gardener, who grafts a number of slips of noble varieties on a single tree; and just as a bee gathers [sweetness] from many flowers, so the concepts of beauty did not remain confined to individual instances thereof, as are sometimes the concepts of ancient and modern poets and of most contemporary artists. Rather, the ancient artists strove to combine the beauties of many beautiful bodies. They purified their works of art of all personal predilections, which divert our spirit from true beauty,[9]

presenting in their works of art neither a likeness of this or that young man or woman, nor a reflection of their own personal taste, but the perfect young man, the ideally beautiful young woman. For, as Winckelmann was convinced, there was in each case only one such ideal. If, according to Plato, artists were engaged in producing imperfect replicas of objects which in themselves were but imperfect replicas of the "idea" of the object, Winckelmann argued that, on the contrary, the Greek artists got very much closer to the Platonic "idea" than any natural object, achieving in this way a pinnacle of "ideal beauty" which the moderns could not hope to rival unless they followed the ancient example: the only way modern artists could achieve greatness was through the imitation of the Greeks.[10]

That "beauty was the supreme law in the works of the visual artists among the ancients," and that the ancients, to a certain extent, "sacrificed truth and expression" to beauty,[11] had become the accepted view in Germany by 1790. It had similarly become a commonplace to assert that the ancient practice was the correct one, and that all art—poetry as well as painting and sculpture—ought to be "beautiful art." In order to account for the "tyranny of Greece over Germany," to borrow E. M. Butler's phrase, we must add, however, that Winckelmann's teachings had joined forces, in a rather peculiar way, with those of Rousseau. As early as 1765, when he drew attention to Winckelmann in his *Salon*, Diderot claimed "qu'il faudrait étudier l'antique pour apprendre à voir la nature"; and when Bougainville landed in Tahiti some two years later, he called the island "la nouvelle Cythère" and bestowed nicknames such as Ajax, Hercules, and Lycurgus on the natives.[12] Thus, Winckelmann's cult of the Greeks began to merge with Rousseau's cult of nature, and if the natives of Polynesia were invested with some of the glory of antiquity, the Greeks, in their turn, received a share of the claims made by Rousseau and his disciples for everything considered natural. By 1790, when Schlegel began to study contemporary esthetics, it was the prevailing opinion that the Greeks were closer to nature than the moderns, and that this was a cause of the superior excellence of their art.[13]

This view was, however, by no means unambiguous. For one thing, it is hardly consistent to claim within the covers of the same book—as was not infrequently done—that whatever is natural is perfect and that the Greeks had to surpass nature to achieve perfection. Much of this difficulty disappears, however, if it is realized that the word "nature" can be used in two very different ways—in Rousseau's sense of "unspoilt nature" contrasted to the artificial conditions of modern life, and in that of "external reality" as contrasted with subjective imaginings. The prevailing direction of thought then emerges as follows. The Greeks, it was held, had the initial advantage of a "natural" mode of existence, unspoilt by modern sophistication, and added to this advantage by improving even on the near-perfect models available to them.

The moderns lived in a depraved environment and compounded this disadvantage either by slavishly copying their inferior models or by indulging in subjective flights of fancy.

Another difficulty was perhaps of greater significance for Schlegel's theories. While Rousseau's cult of nature had been an important factor in the climate of opinion that prevailed during his formative years, the historical perspective of the Enlightenment, which conceived the story of mankind in terms of steady progress, had lost little of its hold on the German mind. Clearly, the question was bound to present itself how the belief in progress could be squared with the belief in the superiority of the ancients. The answer Schlegel suggested is the key to his early writings. It consisted essentially in an ingenious combination of two very different philosophies of history—that of Immanuel Kant and that of J. G. Herder.

According to Kant, history began with man living in complete subservience to instinct, ignorant of good and evil, and in a state of innocence and happiness. Destined to achieve freedom, however, man had to throw off the shackles of instinct and learn to employ his reason: he ate from the tree of knowledge and was expelled from Paradise. In this second stage of his development, according to Kant, man was torn between the dictates of instinct and reason. Having gained knowledge of good and evil, he brought sin into the world; capable of speculating about the future and torn by inner strife, he was harassed by care. For the individual, therefore, man's emergence from the state of nature was a disaster; but for mankind as a whole, it was an advance. Irrevocably, man had embarked on the endless journey toward a third, final, and ideal stage of development, in which man would not only once again enjoy perfect happiness, but be virtuous and free.[14]

Schlegel shared Kant's belief in progress and himself suffered intensely from that inner disharmony which, according to Kant, was characteristic of mankind in its second stage of development. Kant's theory was thus bound to appeal to him. He could hardly fail to notice, however, that this theory was not very easily compatible with the history of the ancient civilizations. Rather, the rise and decline of the ancient world seemed to lend support to the far less optimistic views of Herder, according to whom every civilization, like an individual human being, was destined to pass through the successive stages of childhood, maturity, old age, and decay. Caught between Herder and Kant, Schlegel took from each what best suited his purposes and evolved his own theory, according to which there were two types of civilization, each subject to its own law of development: the "natural" civilization, which obeys the laws of Herder's philosophy of history, and the "artificial" civilization, which embodies Kant's notion of infinite progress.

A "natural" civilization, Schlegel maintained, is one that receives its first impulse from Nature herself; an "artificial" civilization is a creation of the human understanding [*Verstand*]. In the former, activity arises from indefinite desires, in the latter from definite purposes. In the former, the understanding is the servant of inclination, in the latter it is the supreme guiding principle. A "natural" civilization reflects in its culture the beauty and harmony of the undivided human personality and is itself a harmonious whole, whereas an "artificial" civilization is exposed to the conflicts of instinct and intellect, reason and imagination. A "natural" civilization at its best will be blessed with the unique advantages that nature alone can bestow and will thus reach absolute perfection, but for a fleeting moment only; for the dark promptings to which it owes its being will inevitably betray it, so that it is doomed to decadence and extinction. An "artificial" civilization will be beset by all the countless aberrations of the intellect and will remain imperfect forever; but unless it is destroyed by a political or physical disaster, it is capable of perpetual progress toward an unattainable, but infinitely glorious ideal. The Greek civilization was "natural," and the modern civilization "artificial."

In its details, Schlegel's theory is far more complex and difficult than our thumbnail sketch of it suggests, and he himself felt that his presentation of it was not entirely successful. These details are, however, of little consequence, as he himself soon abandoned them. What matters is that his early philosophy provided him with a kind of blueprint of history to which he adhered for many years to come—with the conviction that the ancient civilization was somehow more "natural," if only in a sense of this word that was not always very clearly defined, and that it enjoyed the prerogative of absolute perfection, while the modern civilization was somehow more "spiritual," and enjoyed the prerogative of infinite aspirations and unlimited progress. This conviction underlies the famous distinction between the classical and the romantic which he was to proclaim in later years. In 1794/95, it led, oddly enough, to a troubled, but nonetheless fanatical, classicism.

By a singular coincidence of the most fortunate circumstances, Schlegel asserts in his essay "Über das Studium der griechischen Poesie," Nature had done her utmost for the Greeks. In ancient Greece, art was not an acquired skill, but a natural impulse. Greek culture had never been subject to the errors that the human intellect inevitably commits, but developed "naturally" and in necessary stages, which followed each other by a kind of natural law of organic growth. In the field of poetry, each of these stages gave rise and offered particular advantages to one particular poetic genre, and in each of these genres the Greeks had attained absolute perfection. Thus, the heroic age of the Greek civilization produced the perfect epics—the *Iliad* and the *Odyssey*. The dawn of the Greeks having passed into morning, the Ionian epic was succeeded by the Doric lyric—the supreme lyrical achievement of all times. In the hour of high noon, the Athenians created the perfect examples of the highest poetic genre—the tragedies of Sophocles. If, subsequently, decay set in, this no longer mattered; the Greeks had, as it were, exhausted the possibilities and bequeathed upon posterity timeless models of every legitimate form of poetry: "The history of Greek poetry is a general science of poetry; a complete and legislative model [*gesetzgebende Anschauung*]." "Greek poetry is in its totality a maximum and canon of natural poetry, and every single product of it is the most perfect of its kind." [15]

Not content with asserting that Greek poetry was better than modern poetry, Schlegel—again taking his cue from Winckelmann—went on to claim that it was different in kind. Greek poetry, he averred, was primarily intended to be beautiful, while modern poets were subservient to the interests of science or ethics, striving for truth or virtue rather than beauty: Greek poetry was "beautiful" while modern poetry was "interested." [16] Furthermore, as they single-mindedly aimed at beauty, the Greek poets "idealized"; abstracting both from the peculiarities of individual models and from their own individual predilections, they created works that were "*objektiv*." Modern poets, on the other hand, strove to teach something about the world, including in their representations the individual characteristics of real people or describing real events even when these were ugly; hence, their works were not *"objektiv,"* but *"charakteristisch."* Again, modern poets strove for originality, emphasizing rather than suppressing their personal inclinations, and consequently producing works that were *"individuell"* or *"manieriert."*

Evidently, none of these assertions were very original in 1795; but Schlegel did display originality and ingenuity in making them part of a coherent system. The characteristics of modern poetry, he sought to show, could all be deduced from the simple fact that this poetry was the product of an "artificial" civilization. It was because their civilization was dominated by the understanding, he argued, that modern poets wrote works designed to help them and their readers to understand the world and to increase our knowledge of it; and it was because they lacked the guidance of sound instincts that they could adopt theories of art that allowed them to offend against the autonomy of the esthetic sphere. But such trends, however closely they might be connected with the roots of modern civilization, were aberrations none the less. Schlegel held it to be self-evident that the supreme aim of all art was beauty; he believed that it could be demonstrated *a priori* that "interested" art—i.e., art subservient to the Good and the True rather than to the Beautiful—must be esthetically inferior; and he concluded, therefore, that modern, post-classical art had taken the wrong road.

In calling modern art "interested," "mannered," and "characteristic," Schlegel had by no means exhausted his list of charges. As we have seen, he regarded the development of the epic, the lyric, and the dramatic genres among the Greeks as the outcome of a natural process of organic growth. As the development of modern poetry had, in his view, been much more arbitrary, it was to be expected that the purity of the genres should have been disregarded—an expectation which his wide reading showed him to be justified. While Greek poetry, as he saw it, was an orderly, harmonic whole, modern poetry was a chaos abounding in monstrous hybrids: it was an "ocean of conflicting forces," [17] an "aesthetic junkshop" [18] in which "philosophy waxed poetic while poetry philosophized, history was treated as poetry and poetry as history," and in which lyrical moods became the subjects of dramas while dramatic subjects were squeezed into lyrics.[19] If we add that, according to Schlegel, modern poets only tired of excessive realism in order to rush to the opposite extreme of wild flights of fancy and that modern poetics encouraged misguided practices by erroneous theories, the picture seems hopeless indeed. In his view, however, the very depths to which modern taste had sunk were a reason for optimism. The crisis of the disease had been reached; the heresy of "interested" poetry was about to be cast out, and a new age of art was dawning on the horizon.

In order to make this expectation come true, Schlegel felt, only two things were needed. The prevalent, erroneous theories of poetry had to be replaced by a true system of poetics, to be deduced *a priori*. This, Schlegel was sure, could and would be done, for the simple reason that he was about to do it himself.[20] But the abstract concepts of such a theory would, he felt, be useless unless they were illustrated by examples, and hence modern poets—just like modern artists according to Winckelmann—could only return to the right path by learning from the Greeks. Now of course, as Schlegel himself readily admitted, the Greeks had been imitated time and again in modern times; and this imitation had led to dismal results, for Schlegel shared with Herder and Lessing a strong prejudice against French classicism. But this, he was quick to explain, proved nothing at all. The Greeks had been emulated in the wrong manner—a manner vitiated by a mistaken reliance on Aristotle, and on the basis of a partial and, hence, quite inadequate understanding of Greek life and letters. Greek poetry, and indeed the Greek civilization, was an indivisible whole, in which literature, art, politics, and social customs interpenetrated each other, and in which nothing could be understood in isolation. No Greek poet could offer proper guidance to his modern counterpart unless the latter grasped the whole fabric of Greek life, and hence the imitation of the Greeks was doomed to failure until the appearance of a history of Greek poetry that achieved for this field what Winckelmann had done for the visual arts. To write such a history was, as we have seen, Schlegel's own ambition, and his essay "Über das Studium der griechischen Poesie" was originally intended to serve as the introduction to it. Thus, Schlegel was not only sure that a new poetic epoch—heralded by such writers as Lessing, Wieland, Goethe, and Schiller—was at hand; he was going to usher it in himself.

A careful reader of Schlegel's essay can hardly fail to be struck by a contradiction that runs right through it. While it is full of fierce denigrations of modern poetry, which is shown to be quite incompatible with the laws of esthetics Schlegel postulates, it also testifies to his intense *admiration* of a good many modern poets. Some of these—notably Goethe—were in an exceptional position, as Schlegel found a pronounced tendency towards classical objectivity in their works. With many others, however, no such claim can be made. Schlegel's account of the contrast between ancient and modern poetry culminates in a comparison of Sophocles and Shakespeare—the supreme representatives, in his view, of "beautiful" and of "interested" art. The tragedies of the former, we are told, depend on the "inevitable conflict of fate and mankind," but this conflict is resolved in a kind of "moral beauty." Sophocles' heroes may appear to be crushed by fate but preserve their inner freedom, so that their spirit emerges triumphant. The plays end on a note of harmony, and the spectator leaves with his mind at peace.[21] In Shakespeare's plays, on the other hand, the conflict of mankind and fate is left unresolved; his tragedies end on a note of disharmony, and the total impression they make is one of despair. Now Schlegel left no doubt that it was the "esthetic tragedy" of Sophocles rather than the "philosophic tragedy" of Shakespeare which satisfied the demands of his esthetics; but he nonetheless wrote about Shakespeare with the most fervent enthusiasm. In his essay, he justified this inconsistency by claiming that the methods of characteristic poetry had "provisional validity", i.e., they were the inevitable, and hence legitimate, forms of expression of an artificial civilization until it had reached the stage of maturity that would enable it to embrace the classical canon.

It must be pointed out, however, that the more logical conclusion to be drawn from Schlegel's comparison between Sophocles and Shakespeare would have been that there were two fundamentally different ways of writing, that both had equal validity, and that Shakespeare's way was more suited to modern times. This was exactly the conclusion which Herder had drawn long ago and which Schlegel himself drew when, from 1797 on, he proclaimed the gospel of romantic poetry. If he did not draw this conclusion in 1795, this was no doubt partly due to his early preoccupation with the Greeks and with Winckelmann, but it was also connected with his own personal difficulties. Smarting under his own disharmony, he projected it into his picture of modern poetry. If he singled out Shakespeare as the greatest of modern poets and

Hamlet as Shakespeare's greatest play, this was largely because he identified himself with Hamlet.

According to Schlegel, Hamlet's personality was rent by conflicting forces; he was destroyed by his brilliant, but idle intellect and by the limitless disproportion of his faculties of thought and action. In short, Hamlet succumbed to those very tensions to which Schlegel, according to his letters to his brother, was subject himself. And while he thus interpreted *Hamlet,* and indeed the whole of post-classical literature, in his own image, he projected into Greek literature all the ideals that he longed for, all the harmony and the peace of mind that was denied to him. Greece seemed to him the panacea for his own ills, and he prescribed the same cure to the world at large.[22]

Needless to say that Schlegel's study of the Greeks failed to turn him into a different person. Rather, he learned to accept his inner tensions and to live with himself as he was. The moment he did so, he was ready to accept modern poetry as *it* was, and to reshape his theory of literature accordingly.

CHAPTER 2

New Ventures in Criticism

I *Schlegel and Schiller*

AS we have seen, Schlegel's early esthetic doctrine exhibits within itself the seeds of its own destruction, or at least—as will become evident—of its transformation into the doctrine of romantic poetry.[1] To the historian, who examines Schlegel's early writings armed with the blessings of hindsight, it may well seem that this transformation was inevitable. It was considerably hastened by the fact that a more mature thinker was, at that very moment, proceeding along similar lines. Schlegel's essay "Über das Studium der griechischen Poesie" was sent to its publisher, S. H. K. Michaelis, in December, 1795; in the very same month, Schiller began to publish his famous treatise "Über naïve und sentimentalische Dichtung."

A detailed analysis of this treatise would require a book to itself. Suffice it to say that Schiller also distinguished between two types of poetry—"naïve" poetry, which is the product of a natural and healthy environment and is best represented by the Greeks, and "sentimental" poetry, which is the product of a sophisticated and corrupt environment and is typical of the moderns. The former is intuitive and harmonious, the latter self-conscious and discordant. The former can achieve perfect form, but is limited in its content; the latter is incapable of perfection, but unlimited in its scope and, though inferior in beauty, superior in sublimity.

The similarity between Schiller's and Schlegel's treatise is so striking that scholars have attempted to explain it in terms of direct influence; but the fact is that Schlegel's essay was in the hands of the publisher by the time Schiller's reached Dresden.[2] The most that can be claimed is that Schlegel had read Schiller's *earlier* writings, and had learned from them. What is more important, Schiller and Schlegel were subject to the same intellectual cross-currents and had to cope with the same problems.[3] They both admired the Greeks, both had studied Winckelmann, Rousseau and Kant; and Schiller, no less than Schlegel, was oppressed by the awareness that he lacked the harmony and unreflecting immediacy which were at that time so commonly associated with the Greeks. Moreover, if the two essays resembled each other in some respects, they radically differed in others.

Thus, to concentrate on a few major issues, Schlegel's starting point was the contrast between two stages in the history of mankind, while Schiller vacillated between the systematic and the chronological approach. Schlegel found in idealization one of the salient characteristics of ancient art, while Schiller maintained that the Greeks lived in a near-perfect society and had no need to idealize it. Schlegel regarded all literature written after the collapse of the Roman Empire, and much that had been written earlier, as essentially modern, while Schiller classed a large number of medieval and Renaissance poets as "naïve." Above all, Schlegel praised the Greeks at the expense of the moderns, while Schiller, though he too had yearned for the glory of Greece, not only realized that it was impossible to turn the clock back, but saw no reason for wishing to do so. A better Kantian than Schlegel— though by no means an orthodox one—he not only admitted that the moderns had to pay a price for the prospect of metaphysical freedom which their divorce from nature held out to them, but was confident that freedom was worth this price: he had not only designed his treatise as a vindication of "sentimental" poetry, but had been triumphantly successful in its vindication.

It was this feature that rendered Schiller's treatise so important for Schlegel. When its decisive second installment reached him, he was thrown into such turmoil that he "did nothing for several days but read it and make notes." [4] Two months later, he added a tortuous and confused preface to his essay, hinting at the possibility of a "splendid justification of the moderns" only to reiterate that "interested" poetry merely had "provisional validity, like despotic government." [5] But this was a rearguard action, and his early convictions had begun to crumble.

In fact, having buried himself for two years in the study of the ancients, he now began to tire of such one-sidedness. He continued to work on his history of Greek poetry, but began to devote more and more time to the study of philosophy, further increased his knowledge of Renaissance literature, and kept an eager eye on contemporary publications. This latter interest had the incidental advantage that it could be turned into hard cash: he began to write reviews. We shall discuss these early reviews very briefly, but shall analyze the theoretical principles on which they are based at some length.

Because his interest tended that way, but also for purely accidental reasons, some of Schlegel's earliest reviews dealt with various issues of Schiller's periodical *Die Horen* and with the anthology Schiller edited in 1795, the *Musenalmanach für das Jahr 1796*. Schlegel had not yet outgrown his classicist bias and dealt rather harshly with Schiller's contributions to these publications. Schiller, who had met the young critic in 1792 and disliked him at sight, vented his anger in a number of satirical distichs published in the *Musenalmanach für das Jahr 1797*, the famous "Xenien-Almanach." As, in the meantime, Schiller's *Horen* had descended from brilliant beginnings to a level hardly worthy of its editor, Schlegel had the opportunity of retaliating with a crushing review. At this point, Goethe intervened and persuaded both parties to put an end to the controversy, but the harm had been done: for many years, Schlegel and his whole circle of friends systematically ignored Schiller in their publications, and a magnificent opportunity for fruitful cooperation had been missed.[6]

II Pen Portraits

While Schlegel's attacks on Schiller of 1796/97 are of purely historical importance, his longer critical essays of those years can still be read with profit and interest. At least three of them—the studies of F. H. Jacobi, Georg Forster, and G. E. Lessing, representing a genre which Schlegel called "Charakteristiken" or pen portraits—played a significant role in the development of modern German literary criticism. In order to explain this role, it will be necessary to take a brief look at the kind of criticism written by Schlegel's contemporaries.[7]

For about 300 years—from the beginning of Neo-Classicism to Herder and Diderot—critics had judged poetry by rules, or had at least believed they did, or pretended to do so. By and large, these rules had been abstracted from Greek poetry and were heavily dependent on the poetics of Aristotle and Horace. As an example, it must suffice to refer to the theory of the "three unities," which dominated French neo-classical drama and which was expounded in Germany, with great narrow-mindedness, by Gottsched. Even

Lessing's dramatic criticism, brilliant though it was, depended on Aristotelian categories. Then, just before the time of Schlegel's birth, it was shown by Herder that it did not make sense to expect an Elizabethan Englishman or a German of the eighteenth century to write like an Athenian of the fifth century B.C., and the whole system of rules collapsed.

No doubt, this was an enormous step in the right direction. As a result, however, literary critics, toward the end of the century, found themselves in an awkward position. There was neither a generally accepted theory to which reviewers could refer in support of their judgments, nor was there a tradition of practical criticism which could offer guidance. Lessing had devoted his time partly to reinterpretations of Aristotle that were relevant only within the field of tragedy, and partly to brilliant and very closely argued polemics. He had found a great deal to say about Voltaire, whom he detested, and very little about Shakespeare, whom he admired. Consequently, a critic of Schlegel's generation could most profitably turn to Lessing for instruction in the art of attack, but hardly in the far more important art of positive evaluation and loving interpretation of works of art.

Herder's practical criticism was too rhapsodic, unsystematic, and exclamatory to provide a model, and there was no other literary critic of stature to turn to. Many of Schlegel's contemporaries, as we have seen, found inspiration in the writings of Winckelmann, but in so doing inevitably remained with, or returned to, a form of Neo-Classicism and perpetuated its bias. Thus Schiller, whose private letters testify to the most admirable understanding of *some* aspects of contemporary literature, based his published criticism—e.g., his famous review of Bürger's poems—on a very narrow theory that aroused the ridicule of the younger generation. The bulk of the reviewers had no theory of criticism at all and lived from hand to mouth. The typical review of the 1790's consists of a brief general description of the work in question and of a few phrases of praise or blame supported by a string of disconnected quotations of the best or the worst passages. The modern reader of such reviews may recall Pope's Shakespeare edition of 1725, in which Pope drew attention to passages he liked by asterisks in the margin, explaining that this system "seems . . . a shorter and less ostentatious method of performing the better half of criticism (namely the pointing out of an author's excellencies) than to fill a whole paper with citations of fine passages, with general *Applauses,* or *empty* Exclamations at the tail of them." [8] There seemed to be little awareness that an author's excellence might reside in his ability to create a meaningful, organic *whole* rather than in writing "fine passages."

Evidently, a generalization like the one just made needs to be qualified. There were some critics, such as J. K. F. Manso, who rose far above the general level in a few isolated reviews. On the whole, however, this level was very low indeed until, from 1795 on, the brothers Schlegel and, to a lesser extent, W. von Humboldt introduced more adequate methods and a new approach. It was the elder Schlegel who took the lead. In the three-and-a-half years from January, 1796, to June, 1799, he contributed close to three hundred reviews to the *Jenaische Allgemeine Litteratur-Zeitung,* the most powerful literary organ of the day.[9] "It is far easier to find fault intelligently," he says in one of these reviews, "than to praise intelligently. One can do the first while confining oneself to the surface of a work . . . : doing the latter presupposes that the critic has penetrated the core and that he masters the art of expressing himself, so that he can portray the individuality of a work of art, which escapes mere concepts." [10] August Wilhelm Schlegel showed himself as such a master, and his reviews are not only a monument of industry, but reveal a certainty of judgment and a skill in characterization and analysis that was unique among the reviewers of that day.

Compared with his elder brother, Friedrich wrote very little criticism. He was not nearly as good a stylist and more erratic in his judgments. If he has turned out to be no less influential, this was at least partly due to his more philosophical cast of mind. While his methods of criticism were similar to those of his brother, he employed them with far greater self-awareness, the determination to make them apparent to the reader, and the full realization that they required theoretical justification.

His first major critical study dealt with the philosopher and novelist F. H. Jacobi, whose writings, now almost unknown, were of considerable influence in his own days. In 1796, Jacobi had published a revised version of his philosophical novel *Woldemar.* Schlegel was invited to review it and devoted himself to this assignment with characteristic thoroughness. He read all of Jacobi's works, at first with great enthusiasm, then with the growing conviction that Jacobi's whole *œuvre* was a single systematic attempt at defending his own prejudices, and hence basically dishonest. Guided by this conviction, Schlegel found himself unable to restrict his discussion to the novel he had been asked to review and branched out into a searching pen portrait of Jacobi as a thinker and writer. The result was an essay that was carefully shaped, brilliantly sustained in its argument, devastating in its polemics, and novel in its method.

At first glance, it might appear that this method was nothing but a glaring example of the intentional fallacy. In fact, much of the merit of the essay consists in Schlegel's careful avoidance of this pitfall. After some initial remarks, Schlegel examines the novel as a work of art, showing it to be esthetically unsatisfactory not by the application of external standards, but by demonstrating its inner inconsistency. It is shown that the reader is meant to admire the hero of the novel, but finds himself incapable of doing so. It is only after having made clear that *Woldemar* lacks esthetic unity that Schlegel examines the philosophy of the novel, and it is only when this philosophy is found wanting that he has recourse to something external to the novel, i.e., to the author and *his* philosophy. It was the nineteenth century which has produced the surfeit of biographical studies against which the New Criticism of our days has reacted. In 1796, Schlegel's method of "never restricting himself to one, nor indeed to all of a writer's works, but always, at the same time, to review the whole man," [11] was quite original—an innovation which, as we shall see, he tried to justify on theoretical grounds.

In his essay on *Woldemar,* Schlegel attacked a man who had many friends and few enemies. His next critical venture was in praise of a writer who had been attacked and was no longer in a position to defend himself. Georg Forster—the essayist and writer of travelogues who had invited Caroline to Mainz—had died in 1794. A vigorous defender of the French Revolution, he had been subjected, both before and after his death, to denigrations by political conservatives who, in their search for weapons against him, did not stop short of examining his private life for moral lapses. Schlegel insisted that a writer must be judged on the basis of his writings[12] and demonstrated, through an eloquent and persuasive characterization of Forster's publications, that he had been a man of great intellectual integrity. At the same time, he set up Forster as a classical model of the popularizer, who mediates between the expert and the lay reader and thus serves an educational function that is of the highest importance in modern specialized society. Schlegel's essay probably still ranks among the two or three best assessments we have of Forster.

Schlegel's third major effort in practical criticism similarly opposed prevailing opinions. In the winter and spring of 1796, he had made an intensive study of Lessing and become an ardent admirer of the great critic. In fact, the acerbity of his critical writings at that time is partly due to his conviction that it was his task to continue Lessing's lifelong fight against intellectual sloth and hypocrisy. Now as we shall see in a later chapter, Schlegel had become a determined enemy of that movement of self-confident rationalism which we commonly refer to as the Enlightenment, and of which Lessing had been such a brilliant exponent. However, Lessing had moved with the times and had never become self-satisfied and narrow in his sympathies, while the surviving representatives of the movement had lost touch with the intellectual *avant-garde* and yet—seven years after Lessing's death— were still in control of the most influential organs of publication in Germany. In fact, in spite of Herder, Goethe, Schiller, and the whole Storm-and-Stress movement, public life in Germany was still largely dominated by the attitudes of the Enlightenment, and the intellectual life of the country was hamstrung by men who had once themselves belonged to the vanguard of progress, but had fallen behind and were now devoting their time to the attempt of throwing ridicule upon a new generation of poets and thinkers whose innovations they failed to understand. The prototype of such men was Friedrich Nicolai, the prolific writer and head of an influential publishing house, who had once been a friend of Lessing's and who still took shelter behind the authority of that great name.

It was against such a misuse of Lessing's name that Schlegel turned in his essay. In a paradoxical attempt to show that he had never belonged to the Enlightenment, Schlegel pointed out such facts as that Lessing had tended to believe in metempsychosis and thus should be regarded as a mystic rather than a rationalist, or that Lessing had been an adherent of Spinoza, whose philosophy was held in contempt by the rationalists who claimed kinship with Lessing. Above all, Schlegel tried to show that the protagonists of the Enlightenment constantly talked about Lessing while totally failing to understand him, and that they praised him for the wrong things: Lessing, he claimed, had not been a great literary critic and dramatist, as is universally assumed, but a great philosopher.

It need hardly be pointed out that in such assertions Schlegel virtually poured out the babe with the bath water. Nevertheless, there is much that is valuable in the Lessing essay, and while it is far less convincing in its totality than the studies of Forster and Jacobi, it is scarcely less successful than its forerunners in one very important feature which it shares with them. Its best and most memorable pages are devoted to a pen portrait of Lessing—a portrait which not only exhibits Lessing as the unique person that he was, but makes us realize that his personality was not merely, as it were, a miscellaneous collection of qualities, but an integrated, organic whole, an "individual" in the original, etymological sense of that word. Schlegel himself knew that it was in this feature that the strength of his three essays lay: he referred to them as "Charakteristiken"—a term which played a considerable role in his theory of criticism. It is to this theory that we must now turn.

III   A Theory of Criticism

As we have suggested above, it is one of the outstanding features of Schlegel's essays on Jacobi, Forster, and Lessing that they were written with an exceptional awareness of the critical procedures employed in them. These essays and a number of later writings, such as Schlegel's Geschichte der Poesie der Griechen und Römer (1798) and his "Gespräch über die Poesie" (1800), contain brief excursions into the theory of criticism, and his notebooks of 1797/98 contain numerous jottings on this topic. As Schlegel never produced a systematic account of his theory, it is from these sources that the theory which guided his activities as a practical critic must be reconstructed.

Schlegel's earliest writings, as we have seen, were based on a fanatical classicism that temporarily satisfied his needs as a practical critic. At the same time, however, he attempted to deduce a system of poetics a priori. This attempt, which is preserved in two notebooks with the title Von der Schönheit in der Dichtkunst

(1795–96),[13] was soon abandoned, but represents an important stage in Schlegel's development as a Romantic critic.

Beauty, Schlegel asserts in these notes, has three constituents—constituents which, as it happens, coincide with Kant's Categories of Quantity: oneness or unity, multiplicity or variety, and wholeness or totality. This sounds rather more abstract than it is. By unity, Schlegel meant simply the coherence and connectedness of a work of art which makes it *one* work. (It need hardly be pointed out that such unity could not be demonstrated by the prevalent reviewing method of stringing quotations, so that Schlegel's emphasis on unity as a constituent of beauty was bound to lead him to subtler methods of criticism.) The demand for multiplicity was made initially to ensure that minimum of content or variety without which—at least in the days before Mondrian—there would not be a work of art at all: if we only asked for unity, a black circle on a white background would be a perfect painting. Quite early, however, Schlegel began to exceed such minimum demands and to regard quantitative scope as a virtue in itself. Thus, he argued in 1795 that lyrical poetry was inferior to drama because of its lack of scope, and in 1797 he suggested that it was only a legitimate genre if it occurred within a larger work such as a novel.[14] By 1798, he had come to extol the ideal of all-embracing works or of "Universalpoesie," thus converting a precept resembling the teachings of Aristotle into one that was characteristically Romantic.[15]

Schlegel's "wholeness" or "totality" had, as he himself explained, a dual aspect. With respect to form, it denoted the appearance (*Schein*) of "inner completeness" or "inner necessity"—in short, the critical concept which subsequently rose to fame as "inner" or "organic" form. With respect to content, "wholeness" denoted the symbolic quality of the work of art, which made it an expression of the infinite or the divine: "Beauty . . . is an image of the Godhead, art its language. The artist [is] a true spokesman of God." "Divinity (appearance of totality) is the ruling . . . constituent of Beauty." [16]

The definition of the artist as a "spokesman of God" was to become so essential a part of the Romantic credo that a word of caution seems to be indicated: as long as the word "God" carries no specifically Christian connotations in this context—and it certainly did not in Schlegel's writings of 1795/96—the view of art expressed here is perfectly compatible with the Classicism of Winckelmann or Goethe. In fact, it is so broad a view that it could serve Schlegel equally well as a support for the theories of his Classicist period, as a constituent of his doctrine of romantic poetry, and as a central tenet of the philosophy of art he developed after his conversion. Precisely because of its broadness, however, Schlegel found this view of little use as a practical critic: it was no substitute for the "rules of taste" by which Neo-Classicist criticism supposedly operated, and consequently, whatever value he might attach to it as a theory of art, it was of little avail to him in devising a theory of criticism.

That such a theory was desperately needed was first brought to his attention by his study of Kant, who had shown in his *Critique of Judgment* that there were no laws of beauty, and that esthetic judgments were not subject to proof. When Schlegel first read the *Critique* in 1792, he reacted by stubbornly insisting that there must be such laws, as criticism could not operate without them: "For the creator there are no laws, but . . . without laws one cannot be a *critic*." [17] When he reread the *Critique* early in 1796, his reaction was still quite similar: "A judgment," he now declared, "presupposes a rule. If there are no rules of taste, there is also no taste. He who asserts that taste is entirely subjective denies that it exists." [18] This is of course pure Neo-Classicism; it is the kind of remark that Boileau might have made a hundred years previously. But Schlegel's own taste had by now become too catholic to be restrained by rules. As he read and reread the masterpieces of European literature from Homer to Goethe and gained a deeper understanding of poets as different from each other as Aeschylus and Ariosto, he began to realize that it was folly to search for a system of rules that could be applied with equal justice to the *Iliad*, to *Hamlet*, and to *Wilhelm Meister*. Having reached the point of admitting this, he was ready to face the problem raised by the collapse of Neo-Classicism, and to ask himself the key question which his fellow critics still failed to pose: How does criticism operate if there are no rules of taste?

One possible reply to this question was formulated by Schlegel as follows: "Criticism is not to judge works by a general ideal, but is to search out the *individual* ideal of every work." "Criticism compares a work with its own ideal." [19] These statements anticipate what Benedetto Croce was to preach a century later—that every work of art is *sui generis,* unique and autonomous, so that no laws abstracted from other works can be applied to it. Rather, the critic is assigned the task of discovering the laws inherent in the work itself, and of finding out whether the work obeys these laws of its own; if it does, it has what is now called "inner" or "organic" form.

While the jottings concerning the "individual ideal" of a work which we have just quoted date from 1797 and 1799, the method indicated in them had already been used by Schlegel in his essay on *Woldemar.* An interesting modification of this method is to be found in his study of Forster. Here Schlegel began by investigating what kind of a writer Forster was, what specific social function his writings served, and what his specific aims and tasks were. On the basis of this investigation, Schlegel then constructed a specific ideal for this particular writer—the ideal of the *"gesellschaftliche Schriftsteller"* or "social author" [20]—and compared Forster with this ideal. Thus, Schlegel could rest content that the critical method indicated in his jottings led to a viable practice. He was not satisfied, however, that he had solved his theoretical problem.

In those early days, Schlegel was convinced that it was the main function of criticism to "determine the value" of works of art,[21] i.e., to pronounce esthetic judgments. A critic believing in rules of taste could claim that such value judgments were capable of demonstration. Having abandoned rules, Schlegel could no longer stake such a claim and, hence, was faced with the dilemma of asserting that critics must pass judgment, while having to admit that such judgments could not be demonstrated. His theory of the "individual ideal" obscured this dilemma without really offering a solution, for, as Schlegel was quick to realize, the act of constructing an "individual ideal" did not provide, but *presupposed* a value judgment. It was this realization which led Schlegel to his most radical departure as a theorist of criticism.

In our own century, it has been argued by logical positivists that the judgment "This poem is good" quite simply means "This poem pleases me" or "I like this poem." In 1797, Schlegel came very close to this point of view, but succeeded in avoiding the excessive subjectivity to which it tends to lead. "In pure esthetics," he declared, "one says 'This is how I love the poem', in pure philosophy, 'This is how I understand it'. The question of value is ethical in its very origins." [22]

We can ignore the last sentence, in which Schlegel suggests that "value" is an exclusively ethical phenomenon, as a momentary aberration. It is the first sentence of his statement that is of importance. Here Schlegel suggests, very much like the logical positivists, that we call a work of art good because we like it, and thus admits that esthetic judgments are subjective in origin. He greatly modifies this admission, however, by insisting that these judgments only command authority if their subjectivity is reduced to a minimum.

To begin with, Schlegel explains that the validity of an esthetic judgment depends on the qualifications of the person who makes it: "All genuine esthetic judgments are essentially assertions and cannot be anything but assertions. One cannot prove that they are true, but one must demonstrate one's right to make them." [23] What is implied here is that the passing of esthetic judgments is the prerogative of experts, who demonstrate their expertise by the way in which they pass judgments. Merely asserting them is not enough: "If those mystical art lovers who think that all criticism is dissection and that all dissection destroys enjoyment were thinking logically, then 'I'll be damned!' would be the best judgment of the worthiest work of art." [24] As the critic would waste his time by *merely* asserting his judgments and is incapable of demonstrating their truth, he must aim to persuade.

The tacit assumption which Schlegel makes is that within a given cultural setting the lovers of literature are not wholly unlike one another. Hence, if two persons who genuinely care for literature differ in their evaluation of a given work, this is probably due to their seeing it differently. If the critic succeeds in making his readers see a work in the way he does, he will thereby usually also persuade them to accept his evaluation of it. In other words, the critic does not merely say "I love the poem," but "This is how I love the poem," "This is how—on the basis of my wide experience of literature—I see it." The critic persuades his readers by "characterizing" a poem, by providing a "Charakteristik" or—to give the closest English equivalent—an interpretation.

This may sound trivial nowadays; but Schlegel's further analysis of critical procedure is still of considerable interest. Let us first consider how an interpretation may lead to a change in evaluation. The simplest case is that in which the expert informs the general reader of some facts which he has to know if he is to understand a work of art. Thus, for example, a knowledge of some aspects of Elizabethan demonology may lead to a better understanding, and consequently to a more positive appreciation, of *Hamlet;* or an analysis of the structure of a novel, like that provided by Schlegel in his essay on *Wilhelm Meister,* might lead a reader to appreciate a pattern which he had failed to notice. But Schlegel was not merely concerned with such facts. What mattered to him just as much was the communication of the emotional attitude required for the correct reception of a given work of art, the adequate approach and the proper perspective in which the work must be experienced to yield its secrets. In the light of this conviction, Schlegel laid down that the "Charakteristik" which is the essential tool of criticism is not merely an objective description of the work of art, but a "representation of the impression of the beautiful" or a "representation of the necessary impression" which the work of art makes on the critic; it is this "representation of the impression" (*Darstellung des Eindrucks*) which, according to Schlegel, provides the "absolute esthetic evaluation." [25]

In such statements, Schlegel again anticipated views that were proclaimed a century later as the most recent discoveries. Thus Oscar Wilde claimed in 1891: "The critic is he who can translate into another manner or a new material his impression of beautiful things";[26] and Jules Lemaître wrote at about the same time: "Criticism, whatever be its pretensions, can never go beyond defining the impression which, at a given moment, is made on us by a work of art." [27] Thus, if we have seen Schlegel approach the esthetic heresy of logical positivism, we now see him skirt that of impressionist criticism. Once again, however, it is important to insist on the difference. If criticism could do no more than to define the impression which a work of art makes on us *at a given moment,* as Lemaître would have it, it would be quite useless. Schlegel only shares the subjective starting point with either the positivists or the impressionists and works his way from there toward a new kind of objectivity. What he wants the critic to do is not to define the impression made by the work of art *at a given moment,* but the very opposite: the "pure" or "absolute" or "necessary" impression.

As Schlegel was well aware, the impression which a work of art makes on us is the composite result of a number of circumstances:

the mood we happen to be in, the degree of our acquaintance
with the tradition in which the work stands, the catholicity or nar-
rowness of our taste, and so on.[28] The communication of such a
chance impression would be worthless, and hence Schlegel insists
that the critic must make every effort to purge it of the distortions
caused by the moods of a "given moment" or of insufficient study.
The critic, Schlegel prescribes, must "time and again return to a
work that deserves it, . . . not in order to kill time, nor to gain
knowledge of this or that matter, but so as more precisely to define his impression." [29] He must master both the art of reading
"extremely slowly and with constant analysis of the details" and
that of reading "more quickly and uninterruptedly, so as to gain a
view of the whole." [30] In short, as Schlegel put it in a well-known
aphorism, "The critic is a reader who chews the cud. He should
therefore have more than one stomach." [31]

But even the most thorough study of a work may not enable the
critic to see it in the proper perspective. It was absurd, Schlegel
insisted, to review a single work of an author without adequate
preparation; for the proper point of view on which everything
depends could perhaps only be found through a repeated study of
all his works.[32] Such study, Schlegel hoped, would go far to lend
objectivity to the impression communicated by the critic; but it
would still not go far enough. The critic, he felt, had to strive to
slough off his personal and national prejudices, and could do so
only by the most comprehensive experience of world literature; as
long as he knew only "a part of the realm of poetry," he was
bound to make mistakes—and perhaps he would be more stub-
born in his mistakes if the part of the realm of poetry he knew was
"very large." [33] Hence, Schlegel insisted, only a "ceaseless, ever repeated reading of the classical works," only an "ever renewed
study of the *whole* cycle" could "really be called reading"; nothing less than a "grasp of the whole of poetry and of civilization
itself" could lead to mature judgments.[34] Such mature judgments,
Schlegel felt, would really have objective validity; they would ad-
mittedly result from the personal taste of the critic, but this taste
would have been so developed by the critic's scholarly labors as to
be authoritative. His criticism would not merely be a "poem about
a poem, demonstrating the critic's brilliance," nor would it merely
convey the "impression which the work has made yesterday or

makes to-day on this or that reader, but the impression which it should make on any civilized person at any time." [35]

But Schlegel not only demanded prodigious scholarship from his critic; he also expected him to have at least some of the qualities of a poet. If he insisted that the critic must convey nothing less than the "pure" or "absolute" impression of the work discussed, he was no less insistent that this impression must be communicated to the reader in the most intense fashion: it should not merely be "*mitgeteilt*," but "*dargestellt*," i.e., evoked in the reader with all its emotional overtones. Such complete communication, as distinct from mere description, was, in Schlegel's view, essentially poetic[36] —a view which makes better sense in German than in English, as "Poesie" has a much wider range of meaning than its English equivalent, "poetry." It follows that "poetry can only be criticized by poetry" [37] and that all good criticism is poetry about poetry or "*Poesie der Poesie*" [38]—an unfortunate and obscure phrase which has led to countless misunderstandings: the Romantic fashion of writing poems about poets, paintings, cathedrals etc. is, of course, closely connected with Schlegel's theory of criticism; but it was neither inaugurated by it nor does it form an essential part of it.

As Schlegel now had a viable theory of criticism, and as his interest in literature continued unabated, one is surprised to find that he wrote very few reviews after 1797 (though one of them, his study of *Wilhelm Meisters Lehrjahre,* counts among his most famous essays). To some extent, this may be explained by the fact that his polemical writings of 1796 and 1797 had brought him notoriety rather than fame. A more profound reason is to be found in an aspect of his theory which we have not yet discussed. Already in his earliest writings, Schlegel had maintained that no individual Greek poem could be completely understood in isolation from the rest of Greek literature. As a logical consequence of this view, he had started to work on a history of Greek poetry rather than on individual studies of single works or authors. He had been no less emphatic that modern poetry could only be seen correctly in terms of its historical development, so that here again a view of the whole would have to precede the detailed analysis of the parts. Even contemporary works, he felt, could only be adequately interpreted if there were a clear understanding of the direction in which modern literature was moving or ought to move,

so that the critic's labors were doomed to remain patchwork unless the historian of literature had first done his job. Moreover, he
saw the history of literature not as a conglomeration of empirical
facts but as an organic whole governed by discoverable laws of
development. Thus, according to Schlegel, the critic had to enter a
heuristic circle. The correct evaluation of individual works presupposed a knowledge of the function they performed in the historical development of literature, and this development could only
be surveyed on the basis of an adequate knowledge of the individual works that were its parts. The history of literature could
only be understood on the basis of laws of development, and these
laws could only be discovered by a critical study of the history of
literature. Clearly, then, criticism and historiography were inter-
dependent and inseparable; but if one of these tasks had to be
given priority, it must, on Schlegel's assumptions, be that of the
historian.

In his realization of the importance of history as in many other
ways, Schlegel—though this has never been investigated in any
detail—was evidently and deeply indebted to Herder; but for better or worse, he was willing to go to far greater extremes than his
predecessor. As early as 1794, to quote a few statements at random, he had declared that esthetics was the "philosophical result
of the history of poetry and the only key to it." [39] In 1798, he wrote
that he was "disgusted by every theory that is not historical," [40] in
1800, that "the science of art is its history," [41] and when he obtained the *venia legendi* at the University of Jena in the same
year, he publicly defended the thesis that "*non critice sed historice
est philosophandum.*" [42] In 1804, he called history the "highest,
most general, most natural form of the [human] spirit," [43] and
even asserted that, "history being the only science, the science of
physics must be natural history." [44] In short, he adopted as a general principle that no phenomenon whatever could be understood
except in terms of its historical genesis.

The radicalism of these statements must in part be explained in
terms of the ahistorical attitude of so much of the Enlightenment
—as a reaction against that attitude of mind according to which
"only unreason, not reason" had a "history," reason being and remaining what it was from the beginning to the end of time.[45] His
extremism, however, proved fruitful: while one may smile at the
recklessness of his theoretical assertions, one can hardly deny ad-

miration to the patient, scholarly labors by which they were accompanied, and which helped pave the way for the vast historiographic achievements of the nineteenth century.

Schlegel's first substantial publication was a history—the fragmentary *Geschichte der Poesie der Griechen und Römer,* on which he had been at work since 1794 and which was published in spring, 1798. Today, needless to say, this book is quite out of date. In its own times, it was a major pioneering venture, important not merely because of such individual insights as Schlegel's anticipation of Nietzsche's discovery of the Dionysian element in Greek culture but, above all, because of its approach and method as a whole. Guided by Winckelmann's history of ancient art, Schlegel in this early work was the first, in Germany at least, to tell the story of the growth of Greek poetry in a manner which we now recognize as genuine history—in terms of organic development and unfolding, against the background of sociological changes and with the full awareness that a civilization is an indivisible whole that can only be understood as a whole. It was on the foundations laid by Schlegel that such men as Ph.A. Boeckh and Otfried Müller continued to build, and the influence of his historical method extends deep into the nineteenth century to such men as Dilthey, Scherer, Julian Schmidt, Mommsen, and Treitschke.[46]

If it is typical of Schlegel that he became an important pioneer in virtually every field he touched, it is no less typical that he often moved on to something else before he had achieved more than a fraction of what he had set out to do. The first volume of his *Geschichte der Poesie der Griechen und Römer* discusses the Greek epic at length and breaks off after some ten pages on lyrical poetry. No second volume ever appeared: Schlegel's classicist phase was over, and he had begun to work out his theory of romantic poetry.

CHAPTER 3

The Theory of Romantic Poetry

I *New Friends and Impressions*

IN 1795, August Wilhelm Schlegel left Amsterdam, where he had been employed as a private tutor, and married Caroline; in the following July, he set up house with her in Jena. In August, 1796, Friedrich joined them there, but, prompted by the quarrel with Schiller and a public controversy with K. L. Woltmann, a professor at the University of Jena, left again eleven months later. He now moved to Berlin and rapidly made a place for himself in this city's intellectual life. He became a regular visitor to the literary salons of Henriette Herz and Rahel Levin, made friends with Friedrich Schleiermacher and Ludwig Tieck, and met Wilhelm Wackenroder.

Schleiermacher, who subsequently became the most influential Protestant theologian of his generation, was at that time employed as a preacher at the Berlin public hospital, the Charité. For a year, Schlegel shared an apartment with him. He induced him to write and publish, and persuaded him to take an interest in a much wider range of intellectual activities. In his turn, Schleiermacher passed on to him the results of a more disciplined study of philosophy and awakened in him a more serious interest in religion. Wackenroder, who died in February, 1798, at the age of twenty-five, had written the immensely influential *Herzensergiessungen eines kunstliebenden Klosterbruders*—the first major presentation of a Romantic view of art—insisting that the arts had primarily a religious function, and initiating the Romantic cult of Dürer and the religious paintings of the Renaissance.[1] Tieck, the most prolific, and for some decades the most famous, of the Romantic poets, had already published voluminously. An early novel of his, *Die Geschichte des William Lovell* (1795–96), vividly expressed the fear of nihilism that was to drive so many members of the Romantic generation to seek refuge first in philosophic idealism and subsequently in a return to Christian beliefs. A later novel,

Franz Sternbalds Wanderungen (1798), greatly indebted to ideas of Wackenroder and to Goethe's *Wilhelm Meister,* was vastly overrated by Friedrich Schlegel and is now only read by literary historians. Tieck was a witty satirizer of the Enlightenment and contributed substantially to the rediscovery of medieval German literature and the German chapbooks of the sixteenth and the seventeenth centuries. His dramatic poem, *Oktavian* (1804), has been justly called an *orbis pictus* of Romanticism. It embodies most of the esthetic doctrines and much of the *Weltanschauung* of the first Romantic generation, but does so on a rather superficial level and is now generally regarded as an artistic failure.

Through Friedrich, Schleiermacher and Tieck became acquainted with his brother. To this group of young writers and thinkers—the eldest, A. W. Schlegel, was born in 1767, the youngest, Tieck, in 1773—must be added Friedrich von Hardenberg, better known by his pen name, Novalis, who had been a fellow student of Friedrich's at Leipzig and remained in close touch with him for the rest of his life, particularly during the decisive years from 1797 to 1801. Like Friedrich Schlegel, Novalis was not only a keen student of Fichte but impatient to transcend the rationalistic limitations of Fichte's philosophy. Like Schleiermacher, he had received decisive impulses from Pietism and hoped for a rejuvenation of Christian theology on the basis of philosophic idealism. Though their contemporaries were slow to realize this, he was by far the most gifted poet of the group, and his unfinished novel, *Heinrich von Ofterdingen* (1801), is the only early Romantic novel still regarded as a literary masterpiece.

Even if we omit Wackenroder, who died in 1798, and Schleiermacher, who was not primarily interested in literature, it can hardly be claimed that these men formed a homogeneous group; but they were linked by close friendships, incessantly exchanged ideas, studied each other's private notebooks and published works, and gradually came to share an increasing number of interests, attitudes, and convictions. It may well be doubted that they deliberately founded a movement, but they could hardly fail to be aware that their common opposition to the literary taste and the mental attitudes of the Enlightenment turned them, willy-nilly, into a faction. This faction was held together until 1801 by the organizing talents of A. W. Schlegel and for three years had a focal point in the periodical edited by the Schlegels, the

Athenäum (1798–1800). They never referred to themselves as Romantics. If they subsequently became known by that name, this was due, in a very devious way,[2] to the theories Friedrich Schlegel proclaimed in the *Athenäum*—theories to which they all, to a greater or lesser extent, adhered. These remarks have, however, taken us several years beyond the stage in the development of Schlegel's thought which we have, so far, discussed; we must now retrace our steps.

II   The *"Lyceums-Fragmente"*

In 1796, a collection of aphorisms was published in France that was subsequently translated into German and highly praised in a review by A. W. Schlegel: Chamfort's *Pensées, maximes, anecdotes, dialogues.* When Friedrich read these aphorisms, he was not only enchanted by the author's wit, but enthralled by the informal mode of communication employed in them. He promptly adopted Chamfort's method, but not without far-reaching changes. In his own collections of aphorisms, the short, pithy maxims and observations that are characteristic of the aphoristic genre are intermingled with longer statements, occasionally extending to well over a page of print, that almost amount to miniature treatises. In less than four years, he published three such collections: "Kritische Fragmente," printed in Reichardt's *Lyceum der schönen Künste* and commonly referred to as the "Lyceums-Fragmente" (1797); "Fragmente," consisting of some 300 aphorisms and miniature treatises by himself and not quite half that number contributed by his brother, Novalis, and Schleiermacher, published in the *Athenäum* (1798); and "Ideen," 156 short aphorisms of his own, also published in the *Athenäum* (1800).

When Schlegel wrote the "Lyceums-Fragmente," he was not only aware that he was introducing a new literary genre in Germany, but also delighted in having found a form that was particularly suited to his talents and agreed perfectly with his whole philosophy of invention and communication. While the thinkers of the Enlightenment were inclined to the view that scientific progress, in the widest sense of that phrase, was due to the logical activities of the conscious mind, Schlegel placed far greater emphasis on unconscious processes and flashes of intuition, or, as he preferred to put it, on "wit" and "enthusiasm." He was influenced in this respect by Leibniz' doctrine of the unconscious activities of the monads and, at least to the same extent, by the doctrines of enthusiasm of the Platonic and Plotinic tradition, which reached him directly through Plato and indirectly through such eighteenth-century writers as Shaftesbury and Hemsterhuis. The influence of this tradition on Romantic thought was so strong that attempts have been made to define the whole of Romanticism in terms of a Platonic renaissance.

"Wit," Schlegel laid down, was a product of enthusiasm. It was a "prophetic power," enabling one intuitively to perceive truths which were only subsequently demonstrated. Wit leaped where logic crawled, and it was wit, not logic, that was the "highest principle of knowledge" and the "principle of scientific inventiveness." Now if Schlegel's assumption that scientific progress depends on intuitions, on isolated and irrational flashes of insight or *"witzige Einfälle"* that light up the surrounding darkness like bolts of lightning is correct, it is only a step from there to the view that these intuitions should be communicated as such rather than as parts of a chain of reasoning. The art of plausible assertion, Schlegel believed, was both more difficult and more important than the art of logical demonstration. Wit, he declared, is "fragmentary genius," and its method of communication is the "fragment" or aphorism.[3]

This method offered other advantages as well: it was not only the form in which flashes of insight could be communicated without distortion, but the form in which this could be done wittily; and it was the only form which provided an escape from a serious dilemma in which Schlegel found himself. He was fully aware that all scientific and philosophic endeavor ultimately aimed at the construction of an all-embracing and self-consistent system, in which individual assertions mutually supported each other. Only such a system, he had to admit, could provide man with a true understanding of the world he lived in; and in fact, he himself never ceased to dream of constructing a comprehensive, organically connected "encyclopedia" of knowledge.

On the other hand, he realized the dangers inherent in such a construction—the danger of straining the truth for the sake of consistency, the danger of wilful blindness toward facts that would not fit into the system, the temptation of using a system as an imposing shelter for one's own prejudices. "The most ingenious way of becoming foolish," Shaftesbury had declared, "is by a system."[4] Schlegel's view was more paradoxical: "It is just as fatal for a thinker," he insisted, "to have a system as not to have one. He will therefore have to make up his mind to combine the two." [5] His preferred way of "combining the two" was what he paradoxically called a "system of fragments" [6]—a collection of aphorisms, each of which was formulated so as to create an impression of independence from the rest and which were deliberately not arranged in a systematic order, but depended, in fact, on each other for mutual support and clarification. That such a form of communication created enormous difficulties for the reader was a problem Schlegel failed to take into account.

The "Lyceums-Fragmente" range far and wide, from politics to philosophy and from ethics to literary criticism. They are witty, stimulating, and provocative, and while quite a few of them are obscure, there can be no doubt that many of them would deserve a place even in a very small selection of Schlegel's works. For our purposes, however, it must suffice to quote a few of them, both as an illustration of Schlegel's aphoristic manner and of the extent to which his views on literature had changed since 1795:

My essay on the study of Greek poetry is a mannered hymn in prose on objectivity in poetry. The worst feature of this essay seems to me its total lack of that *sine qua non*, irony; its best feature, the confident assumption that the value of poetry is infinite—as if this could be taken for granted.

All classical genres of poetry in their strict purity are now ridiculous.

From what the moderns want, we must learn what poetry is to become; from what the ancients do, what it must be.

The ancients are neither the Jews, nor the Christians, nor the Englishmen of poetry. They are not the Lord's arbitrarily chosen people in matters of art; they neither possess the sole true esthetic faith, nor do they have a monopoly on poetry.

In the ancients, we see the perfected letter of the whole of poetry; in the moderns, we surmise its evolving spirit.[7]

III *"Romantic Poetry": The Choice of the Word*

The aphorisms we have just quoted show that Schlegel's attitude to modern poetry had changed radically since he had left Dresden. To some extent, this change reflects the results of his extensive study of modern poetry in 1796 and 1797; to some extent, it was brought about by the influence of Schiller, which we discussed in an earlier chapter, and by that of Herder.[8] But the altered perspective in which Schlegel now saw modern poetry also reflects the different attitude he had toward himself. The aphorist of 1797 was no longer the shy and insecure student of 1793 or 1795, but a self-confident young writer who had begun to make a name for himself and had learned to live with himself. Thus, while he still tended to see modern literature in his own image, this was no longer a reason for him to wish to change its fundamental character. He never ceased to admire the ancients and, throughout his life, dreamed of an ideal poetry that would somehow combine the specific virtues of ancient and modern art —the "perfected letter" or ideal form of the former, and the "evolving spirit" or infinite content of the latter. But it was modern poetry which now began to dominate his interests. He was no longer willing to force the modern spirit into the ancient mold, and his dream of a synthesis did not prevent him from advocating, from 1797 on, features of modern poetry that rendered such a synthesis impossible. By and large, the features he now commended were the very same he had previously condemned—the tendency toward the purely imaginative; the *mélange des genres;* the trend toward didacticism, irony, and parody; the fusion of poetry and philosophy; and so on. His characterization of modern literature had become more subtle, but had remained unchanged in its essentials. The critical stance had been reversed.

Needless to say, Schlegel never held the absurd view that all modern poetry was good. On the contrary, he clung to his old convictions that Greek taste had been unfailing, while modern poetry was beset by countless aberrations. He now felt, however, that there was a mainstream of modern poetry—a central trend or tradition—that deserved wholehearted admiration, and that this tradition had to be rediscovered by critics and further developed by poets if modern poetry was to achieve its destiny. Consequently, he set himself the task of defining and analyzing this trend; for if there was one thing he had not changed his mind about, it was his belief in his own vocation to chart the course which the literature of his epoch ought to follow.

In performing this task, Schlegel could make only very limited use of the terminology he had employed in his early essays. He now spoke of the "synthesis" of poetry and philosophy where he had previously spoken of their confusion. He could no longer use such technical terms as "interested," "mannered," or "characteristic," which, in his hands at least, had acquired pejorative connotations; and since he felt—with good reason—that the terminology of his fellow critics was sadly wanting in subtlety and precision, he set about coining new terms and attaching new meanings to old ones, as often as not without bothering to explain them adequately. As a result, many of his contemporaries found his writings unintelligible; his followers picked up his jargon; and scholars have wrung their hands in despair ever since. To provide a complete glossary of his terms would be a Herculean task; we shall focus our attention on one of them.

Schlegel's early writings, as we have seen, centered in the contrast between "ancient" and "modern" poetry. When he attempted to redefine this contrast, the antonyms "ancient" and "modern" no longer served his purposes. The term "modern poetry," as it was commonly used in eighteenth-century Germany, embraced the whole of European literature written since the breakdown of the Roman Empire, including not only countless works that were worthless by common consent, but also whole schools of poetry that, in Schlegel's view, had to be written off as mere false starts, "*falsche Tendenzen.*"

On the other hand, "ancient poetry" included works that were, in some respects at least, harbingers of the modern spirit. Thus, Schlegel had to replace the traditional pair of antonyms, which drew a purely chronological distinction, by a new pair that referred to a difference in essence. He chose the terms "classical" and "romantic." As regards the first of these terms, it will suffice to say that its choice was both unfortunate and inevitable; inevitable because there was no other word that had a chance to be accepted, and unfortunate because this word had two distinct denotations. A work was (and is) called classical if it is a representative of ancient poetry (e.g., *Oedipus Rex*), but also if it is exemplary (e.g., in Schlegel's view, both *Oedipus Rex* and Forster's essays). As regards the second of Schlegel's terms, we shall have to discuss it at length. It will be helpful to begin by classifying the various meanings which the word *romantisch* already had when Schlegel adopted it for his specific purpose. We can distinguish the following:[9]

(1) In the Middle Ages, such words as the Provençal *romans,* the Old French *romanz,* the Spanish *romance* and the Italian *romanzo* were used with reference to the vernacular languages in contrast to classical Latin. This early denotation was retained in eighteenth-century German usage. The word *romanisch,* which is now used in the philological sense of English "Romance," was rare, and it was quite usual to refer to French, Italian, etc., as *"romantische Sprachen."*

(2) As early as the middle of the twelfth century, such words as Old French *romanz* were used with reference to works written in a Romance vernacular. The German *romantisch,* which only began to be used around 1700, retained traces of this meaning, but added to it a chronological significance. In his writings of 1794/95, Schlegel—who at that time was almost totally ignorant of medieval European literature before Dante—used the term *"romantische Poesie"* normally with reference to works written in the period from Dante to Cervantes and Shakespeare. It was quite usual to refer to the age of chivalry as "das romantische Zeitalter." In this sense of the word, "romantisch" contrasts with both "antik" and "modern," but not necessarily, e.g., with "germanisch."

(3) As the poetry written in the Romance vernaculars did not employ classical meters, "romantisch," "romantic," etc. were occasionally used to describe works written in non-classical forms (e.g., in rhymed stanzas rather than hexameters).

(4) Because of the highly imaginative character of the bulk of "romantic" literature in the above-mentioned senses, the adjective came to denote the kind of thing which occurs in romances, *romanzi, romans,* but not in real life. Thus, *"romantisch," "*romantic," etc. came to mean "fantastic," "marvelous," "miraculous," "fanciful," "improbable," "exotic," and so forth. In this sense, the word was used by eighteenth-century rationalists as a term of abuse; Johnson—to cite a much-quoted example—praises Jerome Lobo's having avoided, in his *Voyage to Abyssinia,* "Romantick Absurdities and Incredible Fictions; whatever he relates, whether true or not, is at least probable . . ." [10] *"Romantisch"* retained this connotation when fashions of taste changed and critics ceased to condemn unrealistic, imaginative art as absurd.

(5) As a very high proportion of "romantic" literature dealt with love, the adjective "romantic" itself acquired a vague connec-

tion with love; related nouns, such as German *"Roman"* and English "romance" could, and still can, be used to denote a love relationship.

All these different connotations of "romantic" fitted in remarkably well with Schlegel's conception of the kind of poetry that contrasted in its essence with "classical" poetry. With the sole exception of Shakespeare, all of the authors who in his view had played a leading role in giving modern literature its essential character had written in a Romance language (sense 1). Without exception, they belonged to the "romantic" age (sense 2)—the age before Schlegel's favorite *bête noir,* French Classicism, had, as he was convinced, perverted the great tradition. Already in his earliest writings, Schlegel had associated rhyme with "characteristic" poetry—i.e. with the kind of literature he now described as essentially modern or romantic (sense 3). Totally unrealistic or "fantastic" literature could not, by its very nature, be "objective," and hence was necessarily unclassical (sense 4); and as it was a commonplace that love played a different and much more prominent role in modern poetry, "romantic" could serve as an antonym to "classical" in this sense as well.

All these circumstances notwithstanding, however, it is by no means certain that Schlegel would have decided to replace his earlier expression, "interested poetry," by "romantic poetry," if the adjective had not had a sixth connotation, which we have not yet discussed and which it has not retained: when used in this sense, *romantisch* was felt to have the same semantic relationship to the German noun *Roman* as *dramatisch* to *Drama, episch* to *Epos* and *lyrisch* to *Lyrik.* To put matters differently, when the word was used in this sense, its connection with its etymological origin was felt particularly strongly, but the word no longer referred to the unrealistic *content* of romances, *romanzi,* etc., as in our sense 4, but to a particular narrative *form.* Passages in which *romantisch* and *dramatisch* are contrasted with each other occur very frequently in German writings of the decade from 1795 to 1805, so that in this sixth sense of the word, *romantisch* functions, at times almost, as an antonym of *dramatisch,* a "romantic" work being simply a novel or romance.

In order to appreciate the significance of this sixth connotation of *romantisch,* it must first of all be recalled that Schlegel held Athenian drama to be the supreme achievement of classical poetry. It must also be understood that toward the end of the eighteenth century the German word *Roman* had a much wider range of meaning than the English "novel," or even "novel" and "romance" combined. Much of the original, etymological meaning of the word—French *Romanz*, in twelfth-century usage, denoting a work of fiction in the vernacular—had been preserved, and it was not unusual to apply the word to medieval epics such as Wolfram's *Parzifal* or Dante's *Divina Commedia* and to Italian *romanzi* such as Tasso's *Gerusalemme Liberata*. In fact, the word could even be applied to armchair dramas intended to be read rather than performed, and to plays such as those of Shakespeare, whose form was radically un-Aristotelian.[11] In short, it could be applied to any work of fiction that did not belong to any of the three classical genres—the epic, the drama, and the lyric—in the narrow, restrictive sense of these terms; and, as will be remembered, Schlegel had reached the point where he held that the "classical genres in their strict purity are now ridiculous."

Because of this wide connotation of *Roman*, the word cannot be translated; we are forced to retain it, in spite of the temptation to confuse it with the English sense of the word according to which Julius Caesar was a "Roman." What is important to guard against is the confusion of the word in the wide sense in which Schlegel used it with the narrow sense in which it is the equivalent of the English "novel"—the sense that was already gaining on the wider sense in 1795 and that has since then completely triumphed. This latter confusion has vitiated the critical literature on early German Romanticism for decades.[12] It is only if the wide connotation of our word is fully realized that one can understand why the relationship between *Roman* and *romantisch* was so important to Schlegel: he saw in the *Roman* the characteristic form of the great modern tradition in literature. As he put it in 1797, 1798, and 1800, respectively,

[There are] *three dominant genres. 1. Tragedy* with the Greeks. 2. *Satire* with the Romans. 3. *Roman* with the moderns.

Just as the *Roman* colors [*tingiert*] the whole of modern poetry, so satire . . . colors the whole of Roman poetry.

Just as our poetry did with the *Roman*, so Greek poetry began with, and finally again converged in, the epic.[13]

It was because of his conviction of the dominant role played in the literature of the last thousand years by the *Roman*—i.e., by the rhymed epic in a modern vernacular, the romance, the novel, and even certain types of drama, all considered as variants of one and the same literary form—that Schlegel termed the essence of this literature "romantic."

Schlegel began to use this term in its technical sense in his notebooks of 1797. His earliest public pronouncements on the subject, which remained the most influential ones, are to be found in the "Athenäums-Fragmente" of 1798 and in the "Gespräch über die Poesie" published in the *Athenäum* in 1800. As it is our conviction that Schlegel's theory of romantic poetry underwent only minor modifications between 1798 and 1800,[14] we shall be able to treat the "Fragmente" and the "Gespräch" as expressions of the same doctrine. In the former, the much-quoted *Fragment 116* will be our main source. The latter consists of four short treatises, "Epochen der Dichtkunst," "Rede über die Mythologie," "Brief über den Roman," and "Versuch über den verschiedenen Styl in Goethes früheren und späteren Werken," which are preceded and followed by conversations on various aspects of poetry and criticism. It will be convenient to start with the "Epochen der Dichtkunst."[15] It is here that Schlegel explains what he considers to be the great tradition in modern poetry that must be revitalized.

IV *"Epochs of Poetry"*

Our essayist begins this section of the "Gespräch über die Poesie" with a brief historical survey of Greek literature, in which Sophocles is singled out as an "eternal prototype of harmonic perfection," while Euripides is held to exhibit the first symptoms of the impending decline. These are views which Schlegel's readers had heard before and which were shared by his friends. The Romans, we are told, only had a "brief paroxysm of poetry." Latin satire is praised, but the poetry of the Golden Age of Augustus is described as a kind of glasshouse literature, a forced and sterile flower which foreshadowed the similarly sterile Golden Ages of Louis XIV in France and of Queen Anne in England. The next twelve hundred years are passed over in a few brief sentences.

As Schlegel was not yet very familiar with German and French medieval poetry, he only resumes his historical survey with the late thirteenth century, giving pride of place to the Italians—

Dante, Petrarch, Boccaccio, Ariosto, and Guarini. Of Spain and England we are told that the history of their poetry "is concentrated in the art of two men, Cervantes and Shakespeare, who were so great that everything else, by comparison, appears to be merely a preparatory, explanatory, complementary environment." With their deaths, the flame of poetic imagination is said to have been extinguished in their countries. The age of "wrong trends" had set in:

Out of superficial abstractions and arguments, misinterpretations of the ancients and mediocre talents, there arose in France a comprehensive and coherent system of false poetry based on an equally false theory of poetry; and from France, the imbecility of so-called good taste spread across almost the whole of Europe. The French and the English now constituted their diverse Golden Ages and carefully selected as worthy representatives of the nation in the pantheon of glory . . . authors who without exception cannot even be mentioned in a history of art.[16]

This is the key passage in "Epochen der Dichtkunst." In the first two thirds of the eighteenth century, French Classicism had dominated literary taste and poetic theory in Germany. With the discovery of Shakespeare by German critics and poets, a reaction against this prevailing taste had set in, which culminated in the merciless attacks on Corneille, Racine, and Voltaire in Lessing's *Hamburgische Dramaturgie* (1767–69). Following in the wake of this reaction, Schlegel had already condemned French Classicism in his Dresden writings, where he contrasted the mistaken imitation of individual Greek authors on the basis of Aristotelian theories of poetry with the proper imitation based on a historically founded understanding of Greek poetry as an organic whole. Now he accused this mistaken Classicism of having extinguished the flame of creative imagination and of having ushered in, as it were, a second dark age of European letters. But he no longer contrasted this pseudo-Classicism with a genuine one, but with the great poets of the "romantic" age from Dante to Cervantes, who were not Classicists at all, but had the courage to be themselves.

In the remaining paragraphs of "Epochen der Dichtkunst," Schlegel again repeats something he had already suggested in Dresden: thanks, above all, to Winckelmann and Goethe, it is in Germany that European poetry will find its way back to the right road. The significance of this assertion in his essay of 1800 is, however, the very opposite of what it had been in his Dresden writings. Then, he had exhorted his readers to do what Winckelmann had advocated—to achieve greatness through the imitation of the ancients. Now, he wanted his readers to learn something from Winckelmann which the great art historian had never envisaged. Winckelmann, we are told, had taught us to "see antiquity as a whole" and had provided the "first example of founding an art on the history of its growth,"[17] thus making us realize, as we are to infer, that the moderns were and must remain fundamentally *different* from the ancients: "The science of art is its history."[18]

If the role assigned to Winckelmann is thus virtually the opposite of what it had been five years previously, the same holds true of Goethe. Both in 1794 and in 1800, Goethe is singled out for his unique ability to combine, in his poetry, "essentially modern" and "essentially classical" features;[19] but the emphasis is now reversed. In the Dresden writings, this synthesis had been hailed as a sign of the impending resumption of the classical tradition—not without good reason. Goethe had extolled "objectivity," or, as he preferred to call it, "*Stil*," in his theoretical writings; some of his more recent works could lay greater claim to "objectivity," in the technical sense, than anything else written in eighteenth-century Germany; and he had increasingly tended to publish works that were classicist even in such surface aspects as their themes (*Iphigenie auf Tauris*) or in their metrical form (*Reineke Fuchs*). In the "Gespräch über die Poesie," Schlegel still draws attention to Goethe's "objectivity" and reiterates that his works tend towards that "harmony of the classical and the romantic" which is the "supreme task of all poetry";[20] but the emphasis is now on such romantic qualities of Goethe's as his "universality" or his "progressive maxims",[21] and the work of his which in the *Athenäum* is discussed at far greater length than all his other works taken together is his novel, *Wilhelm Meisters Lehrjahre*.

Goethe's *Wilhelm Meister* has been assigned a key role in the development of Schlegel's theories by a large number of writers on the subject. In view of the fact that Schlegel harshly criticized some aspects of this novel and repeatedly denied that it was a romantic work in the full sense of the word, this emphasis on Goethe's novel seems excessive.[22] What was really fundamental to Schlegel's theories was not his study of any single work, but his sympathetic reading of a good many novels, his awareness that the novel was one of the most important forms of contemporary literature, and his growing conviction that this form was to become increasingly dominant in the future. It was on the basis of this conviction that he plotted the course of romantic poetry—a poetry that had been dominated by *Romane* in the past (the longer works of Dante, Ariosto, Cervantes, etc.), that was now dominated by *Romane* (the novels of Sterne, Diderot, Louvet de Couvray, Goethe, Jean Paul, Tieck, to concentrate on a few names that recur with particular frequency in his writings from 1797 to 1800), and that was going to be dominated by *Romane* in the future (though Schlegel hoped that these would be more imaginative and poetic than the bulk of those works that we ordinarily refer to as "novels"). It was this conviction which enabled him, in *Athenäums-Fragment 116*, to define, in one and the same utterance, what "essentially modern" poetry had been like in the great period from Dante to Cervantes, what it was like now, and what it ought to be like in the future. We shall quote the most important parts of this *Fragment* and add a few words of elucidation.

Athenäums-Fragment 116

Romantic poetry [*Poesie*] is a progressive universal poetry. Its destiny is not merely to reunite all the separate genres of poetry and to put poetry into contact with philosophy and rhetoric. Its aim and mission is, now to mingle, now to fuse poetry and prose, genius and criticism, the poetry of the educated and the poetry of the people, to make life and society poetic, to poeticize wit, to fill and saturate the forms of art with matters of genuine cultural value and to quicken them with the vibrations of humor. It embraces everything that is poetic, from the most comprehensive system of art . . . to the sigh or kiss which the poetic child expresses in artless song. It can lose itself so completely in its subject matter that one may consider its supreme purpose to be the characterization of poetic individuals of every kind; and yet there is no form better suited to the complete self-expression of the spirit of the author, so that many an artist who merely wanted to write a *Roman* willy-nilly portrayed himself. It alone can, like the epic, become a mirror of the whole surrounding world, a portrait of the age. And yet it can, more than any other art form, hover on the wings of poetic reflection between the portrayed object and the portraying artist, free from all real and ideal interests; it can raise this reflection to higher and higher powers and multiply it, as it were, in an endless series of mirrors . . . Other genres have been perfected [*sind fertig*], and can now be completely analyzed. The romantic genre is in a state of becoming; indeed, it is its essential nature that it is eternally becoming and can never be perfected. No theory can exhaust it, and only a divinatory criticism could dare to attempt to characterize its ideal. It alone is infinite, as it alone is free; its supreme law is that the caprice [*Willkür*] of the author shall be subject to no law. The romantic genre is the only one that is more than a genre, but is, as it were, poetry itself; for in a certain sense, all poetry is or ought to be romantic.

By way of comment, it should, first of all, be emphasized that *Poesie* is inadequately rendered by "poetry." *Poesie* is the opposite of all that is prosy, but does not necessarily exclude good *prose*. It is because of this fact that Schlegel could use *romantische Poesie* and *Roman* almost as interchangeable terms.

In defining *romantische Poesie* as progressive, Schlegel did little more than repeat what he had already said in his Dresden writings. The classical genres—the epic, the lyric, and the drama— had been perfected by the Greeks; modern poetry and its main representative, the *Roman*, could never reach perfection, but were assured of an infinite development: romantic poetry is "eternally becoming."

The bulk of *Fragment 116* is devoted to an explanation of what Schlegel meant when defining romantic poetry as "universal poetry." In discussing this concept, it will be convenient to distinguish between universality of form and universality of content.

The classical genres are strictly limited in their form. For the classical epic, the hexameter seems to be *de rigueur,* for the classical elegy, the distich; classical tragedy apparently requires extended choral passages, adheres to the rule of the three unities, etc. The romantic poet is subject to no law. There are *Romane* in verse, e.g., romantic epics, and *Romane* in prose; but, Schlegel holds, what is most characteristic of the *Roman* is the mixture of both: witness Dante's *Vita Nuova,* the plays of Shakespeare, or the countless eighteenth-century novels in which narrative prose is interspersed with poems. And he is not content to state this tendency toward mixing prose and verse as a historical fact, but— forgetting that the romantic poet is subject to no law—insists that the *Roman* ought to combine verse and prose. Quite similarly, Schlegel notes that *Romane* tend to contain epic elements (narrative), dramatic elements (dialogue), and lyrical elements (interspersed poems), and concludes that this is as it ought to be: he declares that the "mixture of the dramatic, epic, and lyric" is one of the characteristics of the *Roman* and that he can "hardly imagine a *Roman* that is not composed of narrative, song and other forms." [23]

In a characteristic passage of the notebook in which he worked out the theory he was to present in *Athenäums-Fragment 116*, Schlegel combined his demand for universality of form with that for universality of content. He distinguished four types of *Roman*—"philosophical" and "psychological" prose novels and "fantastic" and "sentimental" verse novels—only to insist that all these types were inferior in isolation and had to be combined in a single work so as to attain universality.[24] If the classical genres were "pure" both as regards form and content, the *Roman* was "mixed" in both respects—its nature and destiny was to be a *Mischgedicht*.[25] Hence, as *Athenäums-Fragment 116* suggests, it was both the privilege and the duty of the *Romandichter* to portray "life and society" in a poetic manner, to mingle humor, wit, and high seriousness, and to present in the same work both the most sophisticated concepts and the simplest song.

In making these assertions, Schlegel, of course, once again started from historical facts. The classical epic is "objective" in Schlegel's sense—it idealizes, and is presented throughout in the elevated style appropriate to such idealization. In classical drama, "high" tragedy and "low" comedy are kept rigidly apart. Post-classical literature knows no such rigidity and uniformity. The most realistic detail and the bawdiest humor—Sancho's diarrhoea in *Don Quijote* and the porter's dissertation on drink and lechery in *Macbeth*—can be incorporated in works of the most serious intent. And, once again, Schlegel concluded that if these things could be done, they ought to be done, so as to present a true and complete picture of the times and to perform what he considered to be one of the key functions of romantic poetry: to restore the unity which Greek life had and which modern life lacked, to bridge the gap between the intellectuals and the masses, between the "poetry of the educated" and the "poetry of the people," between the practical and the esthetic spheres. As Schlegel tells us in the essay on Forster, "the *Roman* aims at re-uniting our intellectual, moral and social culture with our artistic culture." [26]

Thus, one difference between the *Roman* and the epic is that the former can be a more complete mirror of the surrounding world. Another difference is that it can be a magic mirror. "Nothing," Schlegel tells us in the "Brief über den Roman," "is less compatible with epic style than if the influences of the poet's mood become in the least visible." [27] The romantic poet is at liberty to intrude in his work whenever this serves his purpose. The mirror he holds up to the world can reflect his own image and the world seen from the perspective of this image—the reflection can be "raised to a higher power." And in the tradition of the novel which Schlegel singled out for his attention in the years from 1797 to 1800—the tradition of the comic novel inaugurated by Cervantes and perfected by Laurence Sterne—there is no limit to this process of reflection. Part I of *Don Quijote* is commented and "reflected" upon in Part II; as Schlegel put it, Part I is the "main character" of Part II. [28] In *Tristram Shandy,* Sterne not merely provides an ironic portrait of himself in Yorick, but this portrait of Sterne's *alter ego* is drawn by an interposed narrator, Shandy, who in his role as narrator is also an *alter ego* of Sterne's. Jean Paul, who was singled out for praise in Schlegel's "Brief über den Roman," used even more complex narrative forms; and this whole development reached an almost ludicrous climax in a novel written under Schlegel's direct influence, Brentano's *Godwi.*

Influenced by the structure of *Don Quijote* and *Wilhelm Meisters Lehrjahre,* Schlegel had evolved the theory that a novel should have two centers, like an ellipse. [29] *Godwi* carries this theory to its extreme. The first volume of this work tells a part of the story of its titular hero in the traditional form of an epistolary novel. On the title page, however, it is not Brentano who is named as the author, but one "Maria," and it is with this name that the preface of the book is signed. In the second volume, Maria tells us that he has edited and partly rewritten the letters that make up vol. I on the instructions of one of the main characters of vol. I, Godwi's half-brother Römer. Now Römer is displeased with Maria's efforts and denies him access to further documents. In order to complete his novel nonetheless, Maria visits Godwi himself, who tells him the rest of the story of his life and provides him with supporting documents. In this way, Maria is enabled to continue his task. However, he falls ill, thus reducing Godwi to the status of a character without an author. Godwi takes over, but interrupts his narrative from time to time to inform the reader of the progress of Maria's illness. Thus, the supposed author of vol. I is one of the main characters of vol. II, and the main character of vol. I is a co-author of vol. II. Finally, Maria dies. In an appendix to vol. II, we are told what is purported to be the story of the deceased writer, but is in fact an account of the development of the real author, Brentano himself; and the whole thing ends, appropriately enough, with a poem supposedly written by a character of the novel and addressed to Brentano.

No one who is familiar with the development that led from Sterne to Jean Paul and to such novels as *Godwi* can be in any doubt as to what Schlegel meant when he declared in *Athenäums-Fragment 116* that the romantic author's "caprice" (*Willkür*) is subject to no rule. In fact, Schlegel merely claimed on behalf of all romantic authors a right long claimed by Sterne's Tristram Shandy for himself. ". . . in writing what I have set about," Tristram declared, "I shall confine myself neither to his [Horace's] rules, nor to any man's rules that ever lived." [30] In the case of *Tristram Shandy*, this defiance of rules is directly connected with the unusual structure of this novel, which has no plot in the ordinary sense of the word, but consists of an endless series of digressions. Now to a certain extent the form of *Tristram Shandy* is merely an intensification and ingenious parody of a characteristic which the novel acquired in its earliest days; in fact, it seems a permissible generalization that romantic literature as a whole tends to be more digressive than classical literature. By comparison with the simple outlines of classical tragedy, Shakespearean tragedy, with its intrigues, counterplots, and humorous interludes, seems episodic. By the standards of classical tragedy, the Homeric epics are episodic, but they are very much less so than the medieval romance of chivalry and the *romanzi* of Ariosto and Tasso. No classical author ever wrote a work that can compare in complexity with the elaborate maze of interlocking stories which Cervantes (to refer to a work which Schlegel loved and admired) constructed in his *Galatea*.

Thus, Schlegel had sound historical reasons for suggesting that the author's caprice, and the episodic structure which resulted from its exercise, were characteristic features of romantic, as distinct from classical, literature. In expressing this conviction, however, he did not employ the terminology we have used. In its orig-

inal meaning, "episode" referred to the dialogue between two
choric sections in a Greek drama, i.e., to the main action; hence,
as Schlegel was always keenly aware of the etymological meanings of words and tended to use them in their original sense, the
German terms *Episode* and *episodisch* did not quite meet his purpose. He preferred to use the Greek *parekbasis* for "digression"
and designated the "capricious" structure of much of post-classical
poetry by such expressions as "witty" or "arabesque form," "confusion," and "chaos," asserting for instance that "all romantic poetry
in the narrow sense of the word is chaotic," and that the essential
difference between the works of the ancients on the one hand and
those of Dante, Petrarch, Boccaccio, Ariosto, Tasso, Guarini, Cervantes, and Shakespeare on the other is the latters' *"witzige Kon-
struktion."* [31]

Now at first sight, such terms as "chaos" and "confusion" would
seem to have a pejorative meaning; but this is not what Schlegel
intended. On the contrary, having convinced himself that the best
romantic works from Dante to Shakespeare and most of the best
Romane of the eighteenth century were "chaotic," he insisted that
this was a merit, not a defect. In explaining why he did so, we
hope to be able to show that this view was not as unreasonable as
it might appear at first sight.

In an atmosphere dominated, to a considerable extent, by Kantian philosophy, it seemed plausible to define the beautiful as the
appearance—i.e., as the display to the senses—of a supreme metaphysical quality. Thus, Schiller had defined beauty as "freedom
in appearance," and Schlegel as the "appearance of the good." [32]
His earliest pronouncement on the subject of "caprice"—made in
connection not with romantic poetry, but with Aristophanic comedy—started out from a position remarkably close to that of Schiller:

A person . . . who determines himself solely by his own will and
who makes it evident that he is subject to neither external nor internal
limitations displays complete internal and external personal freedom.
By acting . . . only from purely arbitrary choice and caprice [*aus
reiner Willkür und Laune*], intentionally without reason and against
reason, internal freedom is made evident; external freedom is displayed
in the mischievousness [*Mutwillen*] with which he violates external
limitations, while the Law magnanimously waives its claims. This is
how the Romans displayed freedom in the *saturnalia* . . .

Thus far, everything seems clear: it is by the exercise of his caprice that an author displays his freedom. We have, however, broken off our quotation at a decisive point. Schlegel continues as follows:

That the violation of limitations should only be apparent, that everything really evil and ugly should be avoided, while freedom is nonetheless unlimited: this is the specific task of every such display.[33]

It would serve little purpose to submit this early passage to strict logical scrutiny and to ask how freedom can be unlimited while the violation of the limitations of good taste and morality must be only apparent, not real. Suffice it to say that at least in his later, more mature utterances, Schlegel stated a position that was not self-contradictory, but deliberately paradoxical. From 1794 onward, his patterns of thought were, to a considerable extent, modeled on Fichte's dialectic method, and there was hardly an important aspect of his thought in which he did not advocate a dialectic synthesis of opposites; *not*, be it noted, the synthesis of compromise; not (to borrow a brilliant image of Michael Hamburger's) the worthless kind of balance which is achieved because there is no weight on either scale; not the Aristotelian Golden Mean, which Schlegel ridiculed as "harmonious platitudinousness," [34] but the very opposite: the center which is achieved by "combining the extremes." [35] His whole theory of artistic form is based on such a combination and makes perfectly good sense in the light of it.

What Schlegel wanted was neither reckless irrationalism, nor total disregard of form, nor the kind of poetic action-painting caricatured in a recent cartoon that shows a poet throwing a canful of alphabet soup on a canvas. It was sufficient for his theory that there should be the *semblance* of limitations being violated, of untrammeled caprice, and of confusion; and this is what he really encountered in the best romantic poets and Shandyan novelists. Modern criticism has amply demonstrated that Shandy's apparently helpless drifting from digression to digression belongs to the fictional world of the novel, and that if the interposed author seems to fall prey to every passing whim, the real author, Sterne himself, put these whims into Shandy's head with a deliberate purpose. The appearance of chaos is the secret of the pattern; it is a conscious device by means of which Sterne—among other things—enlivened his work with what Schlegel called "vibrations of humor." [36]

Quite similarly, even though most readers lose their way in the maze of interlocking narratives in the *Galatea,* this maze has been constructed with all the precision of a geometer. And if Schlegel's contemporary critics persisted in seeing in Shakespeare an erratic natural genius, "warbling his native woodnotes wild," [37] Schlegel insisted that he was a highly conscious artist whose apparent digressions usually served a purpose that was no less justified for being far from obvious. In other words, though Schlegel sometimes one-sidedly stressed the "confusion" of romantic poetry in contrast to the orderliness of classical works, what he really found in the literature of the past and demanded of the literature of the future was "symmetry *and* chaos," [38] "educated caprice," [39] an "artistically arranged confusion," and a "charming symmetry of contradictions." [40]

Thus it was only an incomplete statement of his position when Schlegel declared that "the essential characteristic of the *Roman* is chaotic form." [41] What he really envisaged as the ideal form approximated by the great poets of the romantic tradition was the synthesis of apparent chaos and underlying order. It was probably Goethe who drew his attention to the fact that there was a prototype for this form in the visual arts. On his visits to Pompeii, Goethe had been struck by the grotesques with which artists had decorated some of the interior walls—ornamental paintings in which the fancy and the caprice of the artist seemed subject to no limitation, while yet producing a pleasing and coherent whole. In the loggias of the Vatican, he had admired the use to which Raphael had put this form of painting. When Goethe described these paintings in an article of 1789, he called them, however, not "grotesques," but "arabesques." It was this latter expression which Schlegel applied to literature and used to designate the ideal synthesis of chaos and order in this form of art.[42]

V   *Chaos and Eros*

It is one thing to assert that modern forms of literature are more complex than classical forms; it is quite another to claim that this complexity constitutes an ideal. The first is a generalization; an oversimplification no doubt, but one that can be supported with reference to historical facts. The second statement is a value judgment and can only be defended in a totally different fashion. To show how Schlegel arrived at this judgment will be difficult, as his own statements on the subject are scanty and obscure; but the attempt will nonetheless have to be made.

To begin with, it will be well to keep in mind that if romantic poetry is to be "universal" and a synthesis of all simple forms and modes of poetry, then it must of necessity be complex; but evidently, this is a circular argument. If we are to see more deeply, we cannot stay within the sphere of esthetics and must at least begin to probe into some of Schlegel's metaphysical speculations. Let us start with one of the strange and bewildering formulae which are such a characteristic feature of Schlegel's notebooks—a formula which summarizes in a single line Schlegel's central poetic doctrine:[43]

$$\text{The poetic ideal} = \frac{1}{0}\sqrt{\frac{FSM}{0}} \quad (\frac{1}{0} = \text{God}.$$

Stripped of its mathematical or pseudo-mathematical symbolism, the first half of this equation asserts that the poetic ideal is the complete fusion and intermingling of the "fantastic," the "sentimental," and the "mimic." Each of these three terms will require a few words of elucidation.

(1) Already in his earliest writings, Schlegel had insisted that modern literature emphasized the miraculous, fictitious, purely imaginative, and unrealistic to an extent which was incompatible with classical objectivity—in short, that it was *fantastisch*. The briefest glance at chivalric romance, or, for that matter, at Shakespeare's *Tempest* or *A Winter's Tale*, will suffice to indicate what he had in mind. In due course, he had become convinced that creating literature was essentially a function of the imagination (*Fantasie*) or, to put matters differently, that all poetry was or ought to be essentially imaginative (*fantastisch*). (In view of the fact that according to Fichte's philosophy, which so powerfully attracted Schlegel, the world was the product of the Creative Imagination of the Absolute Ego, this conviction assigned a unique position to poetry: the universe is a "poem of the Godhead," [44] and the poet in a very strict sense of the word a Second Maker.) In naming the fantastic as one of the "poetic ideas," [45] moreover,

Schlegel by no means solely referred to the imaginative content of poetry, nor indeed merely to the central role played by the imagination in the writing of poetry. One of the terms which he used to denote the complex structure of romantic poetry discussed above was *"fantastische Form."* It is this last implication of the expression which will be most useful in our present inquiry.

(2) As the reader will recall, "sentimental" is one of the key terms in Schiller's treatise of 1795/96. There, Schiller pointed out that "naïve" poetry was characterized, among other things, by the fact that the personality of the poet never intruded in it, while the "sentimental" poet displayed his emotional involvement in the story he told. Schlegel adopted Schiller's term, but emphatically insisted that one particular sentiment must predominate—that of love.

It will be well to remind ourselves, at this point, that romantic poetry in the historical sense of the expression is associated in most people's minds with "romantic love"; such names as Tristan and Ysoult, Dante and Beatrice, Petrarch and Laura come to mind almost automatically. As F. Bouterwek put it in 1801, under the obvious influence of Schlegel: "The light in which the genuine knight saw his lady and the shadow which Greek national custom cast on all women are radically different—as different as light and shade . . . This difference is nothing less than the soul of post-classical [*neuere*] poetry." [46] One of the earliest meanings of *Roman*—a meaning still in use—is "love story." But while Schlegel and Schiller were, of course, aware of this, it was of secondary importance to them. What mattered to them in this context was not the subject matter of "sentimental" poetry, but the pervading spirit; and while Schiller's definition of sentimentality is complex, Schlegel, for once, is quite unambiguous:

Let us for the moment [he exhorts his readers in the "Brief über den Roman,"] forget the usual, notorious meaning of sentimentality, in which it refers to almost everything that is moving and tearful in a trivial way . . . [The sentimental is] that which stirs us, where feeling predominates—not sensual, but spiritual feeling. The source and the soul of all these stirrings is love, and the spirit of love must hover everywhere, visibly-invisibly, in romantic poetry . . . [47]

(3) By the mimic or mimetic element in poetry Schlegel meant roughly what he had formerly called the characteristic element,

and what we may simply call realism. In his Dresden writings he had condemned realism, since (like the "sentimental" and the "fantastic") it was incompatible with classical objectivity. He now commended it as one ingredient of an imaginative whole, but never ceased to regard the trend toward unalloyed realism as the cardinal sin of the literature of his own times. (Consequently, while Schlegel correctly forecast the predominance which the novel acquired in nineteenth-century literature, he would have been bitterly disappointed by the way it developed; he would have regarded Flaubert as the very embodiment of what he liked to call the "evil principle" in literature, as regards both form and content. He would have deplored not only the realism of the nineteenth-century novel, but its method—the unilinear plot, the invisible, omniscient, impersonal narrator, etc. But he would have hailed such novels as Joyce's *Ulysses* or Thomas Mann's *Magic Mountain* as the beginnings—merely the beginnings—of a return to the great tradition.) He disliked Fielding and called Shakespeare the supreme mimetic poet.[48]

In the "Brief über den Roman," the assertion that the "poetic ideal" is the synthesis of the fantastic, the sentimental, and the mimetic, is not repeated in so many words, but is paraphrased at some length. Schlegel lays down that a work is romantic if it "presents a sentimental subject [*Stoff*] in a fantastic form", [49] and adds that romantic poetry is based on real events:

Ancient poetry is throughout connected with mythology, and actually avoids genuinely historical subjects . . . The [tragic] poet who represented a real event that seriously concerned the whole people was punished. Romantic poetry, on the contrary, rests entirely on a historical foundation . . . Never mind which play you see or which tale you read—if it contains a clever plot (*Intrigue*), you can be virtually certain that it is based on a true story.[50]

It will be noted that one and the same concept—the synthesis of the fantastic, the sentimental, and the mimetic—is singled out both as the ideal of all poetry and as a distinguishing feature of romantic poetry. If it follows that the ideal can only be embodied in romantic poetry, this conclusion may help to explain why Schlegel so often insisted that all poetry should, to a certain extent, be romantic. On the other hand, he was loath to relinquish his conviction that classical poetry was also, in a different way, an embodiment of the ideal, and this conviction could not but tend to confound the very distinction he had set up. The resulting confusion was one he never really succeeded in sorting out. Rather than labor this point, however, we shall pass on from the first half of our equation, "The poetic ideal = FSM," to the second half, "FSM = God." Here, we shall simplify our task by ignoring, at first, one of the three elements whose synthesis Schlegel identified with the Godhead—the mimetic—thus being left with the two ingredients which figure in Schlegel's famous definition of romantic art as that which "presents a sentimental content in a fantastic form."

Evidently, the two parts of this definition are interrelated. We have already seen that "fantastic form" does not denote genuine confusion, but the semblance of chaos, tempered by an underlying order. What Schlegel suggests to us—though, to be sure, he nowhere says so clearly and unambiguously—is that the fantastic form is given a central focus and an underlying order by the "sentimental content," or, to put it more simply, by the spirit of love. Given this form and this spirit, the work of art will be a true microcosm; it will mirror the essential structure of nothing less than the universe itself, which appears to us as an infinite and infinitely bewildering chaos, but which, as Schlegel and his friends never doubted, is an organic whole, the living body of the Godhead, and the expression of divine love. By its chaotic form, the ideal work of art reflects one of the two aspects of the universe which dominated Schlegel's metaphysical speculations throughout all their varying forms, from Fichteanism to Catholicism—its bewildering variety and multiplicity, its wealth of forms, which he was intuitively convinced was infinite—the aspect of *"unendliche Fülle"* (infinite plenitude).

By the underlying order, produced by the spirit of love, the work of art reflects the other aspect of the universe, *"unendliche Einheit"* (infinite unity)—the fact that all the empirical phenomena in their infinite profusion spring from a single source and form an organic whole. In view of the influence exerted on Schlegel by Spinoza and Fichte, it is tempting to identify this principle of "infinite unity" with the former's concept of Substance or with the latter's Absolute Ego; but such an identification would be erroneous. Schlegel's principle is a far vaguer concept, associated primarily with Love rather than Reason or the Creative Imagination, as would be the case with Fichte. And it is not this principle alone, but the *combination* of infinite unity with infinite plenitude in which, according to Schlegel, the Godhead manifests itself. The synthesis of the "fantastic" and the "sentimental," or of "chaos" and "eros," in the ideal work of art reflects and symbolically expresses this combination and thus enables the work of art to become what, according to Schlegel, it must be—the language of God.[51]

Since what we have just said may seem unduly speculative, it may be well to document it with two brief extracts from Schlegel's notebooks. In the first of these, he restates his definition of the romantic as the fusion of fantastic form and sentimental content in the most succinct terms: "The best explanation of the romantic is perhaps *chaos* and *eros*." [52] In the second, he presents his pantheistic vision of the universe as infinite plenitude in infinite unity by reference to the ancient cosmogony that he rejects: "Not hatred, but love separates Chaos." [53] In other words, chaos and eros, fantastic form and sentimental content, seeming confusion and underlying order, infinite variety in infinite unity are formulae both for the ideal work of art and for the universe as a manifestation of the Godhead. If we now recall Schlegel's belief that the romantic poem, however imaginative it may be, symbolically reflects the structure of reality and should, like the *Divina Commedia* or the plays of Shakespeare, hold up a mirror to the age, so that it must, among other things, also be mimetic, we are back at the formula with which we have set out:

$$\text{The poetic ideal} = \frac{1}{0}\sqrt{\frac{\text{FSM}}{0}} \quad (\frac{1}{0} = \text{God}.$$

VI *Irony*

In the preceding pages, we have commented on most of *Athenäums-Fragment 116,* but have passed over a few words to which we must now turn our attention. In the third sentence of this *Fragment,* Schlegel suggests that romantic poetry must combine genius and criticism—"Genialität und Kritik." What is meant by this, and how does it fit in with Schlegel's total concept of poetry?

To a considerable extent, the poetics of the Enlightenment were still dominated by Horace's rule that poetry instructs by delighting. In this precept, instruction is considered the end, delight merely the means; delight is the sugar-coating, instruction the pill itself. With Goethe, Schiller, and Schlegel, art was freed from its subservience to moral instruction. This does not mean that any of them believed in art for art's sake, nor that they regarded art as a mere ornament or pastime, but rather that they were convinced that art itself, quite independently of any moral "wrapped up" in it, performed a vital function for mankind. As they saw it, the delight of art was itself the instruction; or, as they preferred to put it, art was a game, but a serious game; it was essentially playful, but also essentially serious—"*ein ernster Scherz.*" [54]

Thus, art was to them essentially a paradox, and Schlegel never tired of defining and redefining the paradoxical nature and function of art in a hundred ways. It was, to him, the dialectic fusion not of one pair of opposites, but of many pairs, all of which, shading off into each other in subtle nuances, were the periphery, as it were, of the same mysterious center that was the heart of the paradox. Playfulness and seriousness, intuition and circumspection, the self-intoxication of genius and critical detachment, "sentimental," metaphysical content and "fantastic," witty form—all these he regarded as different aspects of the same phenomenon, the essential "duplicity" of art, which reflected the "duplicity" of man[55] and the duplicity—the infinite plenitude and infinite unity—of the world itself. But in order to produce such art, the artist himself must be in a paradoxical frame of mind; he himself must be both detached and involved, deeply serious about his art and yet capable of treating it as a mere game, trustful of his deepest impulses and yet full of critical, conscious awareness:

In every good poem, everything must be intentional, and everything must be instinctive . . .[56]

So as to be able to write well about a topic, one must no longer be interested in it; the thought which one is to express with circumspection must already be completely past, one must no longer be really concerned with it. As long as the artist invents and is inspired, he has, at least for purposes of communication, no freedom. He will want to say everything; and that is a false tendency of young geniuses, or a genuine prejudice of old bunglers. The artist thus fails to recognize the value and the dignity of self-limitation, which, for him as for everyone else, is the Alpha and Omega, the most essential thing and the most sublime. The most essential: for, wherever one does not limit oneself, he is limited by the world and becomes a slave. The most sublime: for one can only limit himself . . . where one has infinite strength, self-creation and self-destruction. Even a conversation among friends that cannot be broken off at any moment, out of sheer caprice, has a certain lack of freedom . . . Only three errors are to be avoided. What seems and ought to seem sheer caprice . . . must yet at bottom be also absolutely necessary and rational; otherwise whim turns into obstinacy, the artist becomes unfree, and self-limitation becomes self-destruction. Secondly: one must not limit oneself too hurriedly, and allow time for self-creation, invention, and enthusiasm to run their full course. Thirdly: one must not overdo self-limitation.[57]

There are artists who—though they do not think too highly of art, this being impossible—are not free enough to rise even above their highest ideal.[58]

We must rise above our own love and be able to destroy in our thoughts what we adore; if we cannot do this, we lack—irrespective of what other abilities we may have—the feeling for [*Sinn für*] the universe.[59]

But what is that frame of mind that enables the artist to combine inspiration and self-criticism, caprice and conscious control, idealism and the knowledge that his highest ideals still fall infinitely short of man's destiny? In one of his aphorisms, Schlegel suggested that the "self-limitation" praised in *Lyceums-Fragment* 37 was the result of "self-creation" and "self-destruction"; in another, he identified the "constant alternation of self-creation and self-destruction" with the very concept for which we have been searching: *irony.*[60]

The word which Schlegel thus applied to literature and which he bent to his own purposes with such success that some of his most original formulations seem to us, one hundred and sixty years later, almost trivial, had its origin in philosophy. In the Socratic dialogues the Greek word *"eironeia"* is used in its original meaning of "feigned ignorance." But, as Schlegel knew, Socrates had not merely pretended to be ignorant. His *"eironeia"* had not been the straightforward rhetorical device that consists of saying the opposite of what is meant: when Socrates asserted that he knew nothing, he not only knew more than his interlocutor, but knew enough to know that he did not really know anything properly, so that his assertion was both true and false. It was "ironic" because it was profoundly ambiguous; and it is this ambiguity that Schlegel insisted on in his earliest definitions of irony:

Socratic irony . . . is intended to deceive none but those who consider it to be deceptive . . . In it, everything should be both playful and serious, both frank and obvious and yet deeply hidden . . . [Irony] is the freest of all licenses, for through it one rises above one's own self; and it is also the most circumscribed, for it is absolutely necessary.[61]

If this definition applies almost equally well to certain aspects of Schlegel's concept of romantic poetry, this is no accident. The romantic poet—as seen by Schlegel—also claims to know more than the common man, while knowing enough to realize that his most inspired insight is, like all finite things, wholly inadequate. Professing an art which is "eternally becoming" and never perfect, he knows that he is doomed to perpetual failure; but by the ironic admission of failure within the work itself the failure is nullified. The work can never more than partially and imperfectly express the poet's "feeling for the universe"; but by the ironic depreciation of the work within the work—the admission that it is merely a serious game—this deficiency is compensated:

[Socratic irony] contains and arouses a feeling of the irresolvable conflict of the limitless and the limited, of the impossibility and the necessity of complete communication.[62]

Irony is, as it were, the demonstration [ἐπίδειξις] of infinity, of universality, of the feeling for the universe.[63]

The actual homeland of irony is philosophy . . . Poetry alone can rise to the heights of philosophy in this respect and is not limited to ironic passages, like rhetoric. There are ancient and modern poems that breathe the divine spirit of irony throughout, as a whole, and everywhere. There is in them a truly transcendental buffoonery. In their spirit [im Innern], the mood which surveys everything and rises infinitely above everything that is limited, even above one's own art, virtue, or genius; in their externals [im Äußern], in their execution, the mimic manner of an ordinary good Italian buffo.[64]

The reference to the clown of the *commedia dell'arte* at the end of this passage has puzzled critics, but is not really obscure; it takes us straight back to some of the most characteristic features of the kind of literature that Schlegel called romantic. When Laurence Sterne—to use the most obvious example—composes his *Tristram Shandy* with conscious deliberation while the interposed narrator displays untrammelled caprice, the relationship between them is ironic in the full sense of the word. When that narrator advises a reader to skip the rest of a chapter and then shouts after him to shut the door quietly, as if the reader were a listener leaving the room; when he instructs another reader to go through a chapter for a second time and with greater care; when he inserts a dedication into the middle of the novel and proposes to auction it off to the highest bidder; when he starts a digression in order to apologize for a digression, to mention only a few of the hundreds of passages in which Shandy dons Yorick's cap, this is buffoonery. And it is "*transcendental* buffoonery" in a very precise, though highly technical sense: in *Athenäums-Fragment 238,* Schlegel explains that what he calls "transcendental poetry" is characterized by those constant reflections of the work of art in the work of art itself that are such a prominent feature of Sterne's technique.[65]

It is striking how many of Schlegel's countless definitions of irony apply quite literally to Sterne's narrative manner. Thus, Schlegel defined irony as "constant self-parody," [66] and Sterne's interposed narrator constantly parodies his own method of narration. Schlegel defined irony as a "permanent digression," and *Tristram Shandy* is a system of such digressions. He defined irony as the "consciousness of the . . . infinitely full chaos," [67] and the chaotic form of Sterne's novel is the very way in which, according to Schlegel, the "infinite plenitude" of the universe is reflected in the romantic work of art. But, of course, *Tristram Shandy* is only a particularly obvious example of what Schlegel had in mind. A similar case could be made for the novels of Jean Paul,[68] and for any novel in which the technique of the interposed narrator is used for humorous purposes. Schlegel himself pointed out the irony in *Wilhelm Meisters Lehrjahre* and the parodistic features of the Italian *romanzo.* And irony is by no means confined to narrative fiction: when Shakespeare, whom Schlegel considered a master of irony, makes his Othello utter a pun at the very moment when he prepares to murder his wife—"Put out the light, and then put out the light"—he displays the very fusion of involvement and detachment, of seriousness and playfulness, in which Schlegel saw the essence of irony.

In Schlegel's view, irony could not but be present in any product of the human mind that displayed adequate awareness of the paradoxical position of mankind itself. As early as 1792, he had written to his brother that "whoever is not, in the consciousness of his infinite power, pervaded [durchdrungen] with the feeling of his insignificance, must be a little shortsighted." [69] Five years later, he had come to understand that it was through irony that one learned to keep sight of this awareness without being crushed by it,[70] and that, consequently, irony was obligatory.[71] Irony, as he now knew, was the "form of the paradoxical," and everything was paradoxical that was "at once great and good." [72]

Needless to say, our brief remarks on Schlegel's concept of irony cannot claim to do justice to a subject which has been argued about at great length by generations of scholars;[73] nor can it be claimed that Schlegel himself provided a systematic analysis. His comments on the subject in 1797/98 are stimulating and provocative rather than methodical; and after that he used the term much more sparingly. It was his achievement, however, to have introduced the term irony into modern literary criticism[74] and to have started the long and intensive discussion of its nature and significance—a discussion that has been going on ever since and is by no means concluded.

VII *Poetry and Philosophy*

So far, we have discussed only two of the four main sections of the "Gespräch über die Poesie": "Epochen der Dichtkunst" and "Brief über den Roman." All that need be said in the present context about the "Versuch über den verschiedenen Styl in Goethes früheren und späteren Werken" is that this first attempt to distinguish different stages in Goethe's development as a poet has stood the test of time. The "Rede über die Mythologie" will have to be discussed in greater detail. Before this can be done, however, we shall have to turn to a topic which we have barely touched upon —Schlegel's development as a philosopher.[75]

Like that other famous son of a Protestant clergyman, Friedrich Nietzsche, the young Schlegel had reacted sharply against his fa-

ther's faith. The Protestant theology of his own times seemed to
him shallow and insincere, and he delighted in Lessing's attacks
on it. To satisfy his metaphysical needs—that "thirst for the infinite" of which he writes so frequently in his early letters—he had
turned to Plato, whom he never ceased to admire, and to Kant,
whose philosophy stimulated his thought in many ways, but failed
to convince him. In 1795 he began to read Fichte, whom he soon
came to regard as the greatest philosopher of the epoch and one
of the greatest philosophers of all times. What impressed him so
greatly was, for one thing, the powerful personality that revealed
itself in Fichte's writings. "The greatest metaphysical thinker now
alive," Schlegel confided to his brother in August, 1795, "is a very
popular writer . . . Compare the ravishing eloquence of this man
in his *Lectures on the Vocation of the Scholar* with Schiller's styl-
ized exercises in rhetoric. He is such a one for whom Hamlet
sighed in vain; every trait of his public life seems to say: this is a
man." [76] Still more important was the fact that Fichte's *Theory of
Science* seemed to provide the answer to a problem which Kant,
in Schlegel's view, had failed to solve—the steadily increasing
threat of materialism which had developed in the wake of the
triumphal march of science.

The first major breakthrough of modern science had come in
mechanics, e.g., in the discovery of the laws of falling bodies and,
more spectacularly, in the "celestial mechanics" that explained the
motion of the planets. In due course, mechanics and its technolog-
ical counterpart, the machine, inevitably became the dominant
model of thought. In his famous lecture on the circulation of the
blood of 1628, Harvey described the heart as a "piece of machin-
ery in which one wheel gives motion to another"; the blood, he
told his listeners, is pushed through the heart "as by two clacks of
a water bellows to raise water." Some fifty years later, Nehemiah
Grew, the botanist, declared that "all nature is as a great Engine,
made by, and held in His [God's] hands." Robert Boyle, the
chemist, summed up:

God established those rules of motion, and that order among things
corporeal, which we call the Laws of Nature. Thus, the universe being
once framed by God, and the Laws of Motion settled, the mechanical
philosophy teaches that the phenomena of the world are physically produced by the mechanical properties of the parts of matter. [77]

Now the phenomena of the world which thus fall under the iron law of mechanical causation include not only such objects as stars or projectiles, but plants, animals, and our own selves. Early in the seventeenth century, Descartes had been driven by the logic of his own arguments to assert that the human body should be considered "as a kind of machine, so made up . . . that even if there were in it no mind, it would still exhibit the same motions which it manifests at present . . ." [78] Animals, according to Descartes, were simply automata; human beings would be, were it not for the human soul, which was free, and was the source of voluntary actions. In this way, Descartes avoided the denial of free will and all the difficulties that would accrue from such a denial. But the concept he drew on for this purpose—the soul, which he located in the pineal gland—was itself one that had very poor credentials in the eyes of "enlightened" thinkers: the only evidence for its existence independent of the body was authority, and Descartes's notion that it freely initiated bodily actions was incompatible with the principle of mechanical causation. Diderot severely scolded Hemsterhuis for using the very word "soul," which, Diderot was convinced, had no intelligible meaning whatever.[79] Thus, the new manner of thinking inevitably tended to suggest that free will, and hence moral responsibility, were mere illusions.

In consequence, some of the more farsighted thinkers of Schlegel's generation, who inherited the problems of the "mechanical philosophy" but had come too late to share in the excitement engendered by the tremendous achievements of modern science from Copernicus to Newton, began to feel that the very foundations of human conduct and social cohesion were in danger of collapsing. The influence of British empiricist philosophers such as Locke and Hume, though not very far-reaching, tended to intensify rather than allay their fear of nihilism—a fear perhaps most clearly expressed in Tieck's early novel, *William Lovell*. As Friedrich Schlegel put it in 1796, expressing at the same time both the problem that beset him and the direction in which he hoped for a solution, "From the point of view of the consistent empiricist, everything divine, dignified, sacred, great, sublime etc. is *nonsense*. All this is really *mystical*." "It is really the mystics from whom we must now learn philosophy." "The *nature* and starting

point [of mysticism] is the arbitrary positing of the absolute."
"Spinoza is the best mystic known to us before Fichte." [80]

Of course, Fichte would have been appalled if he had known
that he figured in Schlegel's philosophical notebooks as a mystic
(and indeed, in spite of the passages just quoted, the term implies
criticism as well as praise in Schlegel's usage of 1796). But there is
no doubt that Fichte's philosophy was, in almost every respect,
the very opposite of the rational empiricism of the mechanists and
materialists. If they tended to believe in the primacy of matter,
Fichte denied that it had any reality; if they attempted to found
all knowledge on empirical evidence, Fichte strove to erect a system that was purely deductive; if they based science on the concept of strict causation, his key concept was Freedom; and if at
least some of them managed to combine the mechanical philosophy with theist beliefs, Fichte evolved a form of ethical pantheism
that rigidly excluded the possibility of a personal God. Thus,
Schlegel found in his philosophy a magnificent vindication of the
dignity of man, the intellectual courage and honesty that seemed
lacking to him in almost every other quarter, and—as he was
quick to grasp the possibilities of Fichte's dialectic—a new and, it
seemed to him, vastly superior method of philosophizing. In 1797,
he paid public homage to Fichte in a perspicacious review.[81] One
year later, he extolled Fichte's *Theory of Science,* along with the
French Revolution and Goethe's *Wilhelm Meister,* as one of "the
greatest trends of the age." [82] Yet almost from the start, his admiration of Fichte was tempered by criticism.

As we have seen, Schlegel's philosophical endeavors were
guided by two vague but powerful concepts: that of the "absolute
unity" of the universe and that of its "infinite plenitude" or variety. Fichte's radical monism agreed perfectly with the first of
these principles and went far to satisfy the "thirst for the infinite"
that was so powerful an expression of Schlegel's metaphysical
longings. But Fichte's system hardly allowed for the other principle, to which Schlegel adhered with equal tenacity. Whereas to
Fichte, Nature was merely the "non-ego," a mere obstacle in
man's way to Freedom or a mere field for his activity, Schlegel
endowed Nature with a life of its own and denied causality with a
radicalism that bordered on the absurd, holding that "nothing is
real in the world that is not alive," that "all motion is individual

and dynamic," that "all motion is instinct," and that consequently, for instance, "rivers do not mechanically fall into the ocean, but organically strive towards it." [83]

In attempting to go beyond Fichte's *Theory of Science*, Schlegel moved, for a number of years, along lines of investigation pursued at that time also by Schelling—with the result that the two thinkers subsequently accused each other of plagiarism. They both felt that it must be possible somehow to combine Spinoza's dogmatism with Fichte's idealism in a new "Ideal-Realismus" that would avoid the weaknesses of either system. Schlegel, in particular, felt that Fichte's mistake had been not to have pursued his argument far enough, and that Idealism, if pressed to its conclusion, would itself give rise to a "new limitless Realism." [84] In order that this might be brought about, however, Schlegel held that philosophy would have to be supplemented by poetry; the former, with its tools of reason and logic, would establish the idealistic aspect of the universe and demonstrate its ultimate oneness, while the latter, drawing on imagination and inspiration as its source of knowledge, established the realistic aspect and enabled us to surmise its infinite plenitude: "What can be done as long as philosophy and poetry are separated, has been done and perfected: therefore the time has come to combine the two." [85] The combination of poetry and philosophy, it will be recalled, had been demanded by Schlegel already in 1798 as an aspect of the universality of romantic poetry. Subsequently he came to feel that by effecting this combination, romantic poetry came to fulfill a specific religious function.

From 1797 on, the subject of religion had been pressed on his attention from many sides. Lessing's famous pamphlet, *Die Erziehung des Menschengeschlechts*, which Schlegel had studied in connection with his essay on Lessing, drew his attention to the notion of a "progressive" Christianity that would culminate in a third revelation, supplanting traditional Christian ethics with its motivation through rewards and punishments by an ethic based on moral virtue as an end in itself. Hemsterhuis, whom he reread in 1797/98, employed the idea of a synthesis of poetry and philosophy in the defense of deism. Schlegel's friend Novalis, with whom he exchanged notebooks, was drawing on Fichtean ideas in support of his own, basically Christian convictions. Above all,

Schleiermacher, with whom he shared an apartment in 1798, was engaged in an ambitious attempt to make Christianity intellectually respectable in the eyes of skeptics who were repulsed by the stratagems of the run-of-the-mill theologians of the day. In his *Reden über die Religion,* published anonymously in 1799, he advocated a concept of religion stripped of all dogmatic content and consisting basically of a specific kind of emotion. The essential nature of religion, he asserted, was "neither thought nor action, but intuition [*Anschauung*] and feeling." Deciding on the right course of action was an "art," speculation was "science," religion a "feeling and taste for the infinite," an "intuition of the universe." [86]

As a result of these influences, among which his reading of Lessing and his conversations with Schleiermacher were probably the most important, Schlegel had planned as early as October, 1798, to "write a new Bible and follow in the footsteps of Mohammed and Luther." [87] In the end, he produced something far less ambitious—a collection of aphorisms, published in 1800 under the title "Ideen." [88] In marked contrast to Schlegel's earlier aphorisms, this third and last collection is somewhat monotonously centered on a single idea—the interdependence of poetry, philosophy, and religion. Quoting some of the aphorisms will be more useful than an attempt to summarize them:

The understanding, says the author of the *Speeches on Religion,* knows only of the Universe; let the imagination rule, and you have a God. Quite right! The imagination is man's organ for the Godhead.

It is only through religion that logic turns into philosophy . . .

Only he can be an artist who has a religion of his own, an original view of the infinite.

He who has religion, will speak poetry; but the tool to search for it and to discover it is philosophy.

What man is among the other phenomena [*Bildungen*] of the earth, that is the artist among men.

Depending on the point of view, poetry and philosophy are different spheres, different forms, or the factors of religion; for if you really attempt to combine the two, you will get nothing but religion.

Where philosophy ceases, poetry must begin . . .

One has only as much virtue [*Moral*] as he has philosophy and poetry.

All philosophy is Idealism, and there is no true Realism but that of poetry. But poetry and philosophy are only extremes. It is quite true to say that some people are pure Idealists and others decided Realists; but that only means that there are as yet no fully developed minds, there is as yet no religion.[89]

If it is objected to such utterances that they are mere verbal fireworks and that they offer the shadow of religion instead of its substance, it will be well to admit that such a shadow was all that Schlegel as yet possessed. Even so, the main import of the "Ideen" is clear enough. By their insistence on art and the imagination as tools of discovery and as means of communication, they not only highlight Schlegel's defiance of the most sacred tenets of the Enlightenment, but indicate the extent to which he had emancipated himself from the methods and teachings of Fichte's theory of science. The "Ideen" also suggest the way in which Schlegel's search for a new concept of religion forced him to clarify certain aspects of his theory of poetry. He had always held that all genuine poetry was symbolic; in saying, in the "Ideen," that "he who has religion will speak poetry," he had merely paraphrased his earlier, Platonic conviction that the artist was the spokesman of the Godhead. When he added, however, that "in the world of language, religion appears necessarily as mythology or as a Bible,"[90] he began to indicate the way in which he thought the artist might perform this function. It is this subject that he took up in his "Rede über die Mythologie."

Greek mythology, Schlegel suggests in this essay, had provided the poets and artists of antiquity with a common symbolic language. Because of this common stock of symbols, all the poems of antiquity were part of one and the same total structure: "Ancient poetry [is] one single indivisible complete poem."[91] This mythology, he continued, was the product of a youthful, untutored imagination, but it was not mere fancy; on the contrary—the reader had only to view it in the light of the teachings of Spinoza and of the most recent, romantic, Schellingian philosophy of nature to realize that it was based on, and expressed, insights of fundamental importance. Ancient mythology was a symbolic representation of a universe in which there was no dead matter, but which was, in its entirety, organic and alive. Consequently, as Schlegel invites us to read between the lines of his essay, this mythology was not only great poetry, but better science than that of the empiricists. "All physics which is not directed towards astrology," he jotted down in his notebook, "is trivial . . . The method of the physicist must be historical—his ultimate aim mythology." [92]

Modern poets and artists, Schlegel continued, had no such common symbolism, and hence every modern poem was a totally fresh start, "like a new creation *ex nihilo*." [93] The remedy, however, was at hand. All that was needed was the revitalization of mythology—not of that of classical antiquity only, but of the mythology of all peoples and all times—and its conscious and deliberate transformation into a new symbolic structure, which, in contrast to the earlier, "natural" mythologies, would be "the most artful of all works of art." [94] Contemporary physics—a term with which Schlegel referred both to such recent discoveries as galvanism and "animal magnetism" and to deductive systems of science in the manner of Schelling—had begun to open up new ways to knowledge. If poets could be persuaded to take part in this new quest for understanding, the possibilities were unlimited.

Be worthy of the greatness of your age, [he exhorted his listeners] and the fog will be lifted from your eyes . . . All thinking is divination, but man is only just beginning to become aware of his divinatory powers. To what immeasurable degree will these powers still be increased—and that even now! It seems to me that if one were to understand the age, i.e., that great process of general rejuvenation [which is now taking place] . . . , he must be able to succeed in grasping the poles of mankind and in knowing and understanding the deeds of earliest man and the character of the Golden Age that is yet to come.[95]

Needless to say, these high hopes, which are so characteristic of the spirit in which the early Romantics greeted the dawn of the nineteenth century, remained unfulfilled. The poetry that was to elevate the Romantic philosophy of nature into a new mythology remained unwritten, and the philosophy itself turned out to be a false start. The deductive systems failed to produce new knowledge, and those lines of research which, according to Romantic expectations, were about to prove that all substance was organic and alive, ultimately led in the opposite direction—that of an ever increasing dominance of the methods of empiricism and the principle of causation. Romantic science degenerated into the amateurish investigation of water diviners, prophetic peasants, and stigmatized nuns. As for Schlegel himself, less than a decade passed before he had decided that the eternal verities of Catholicism rendered a new mythology unnecessary.

VIII "A Romantic Book"

Because of the long section on mythology in the "Gespräch über die Poesie," it has been suggested that Schlegel's theory of 1800 is, after all, somewhat different from that of 1798: in 1798, the *Roman* is supposed to be the decisive characteristic of romantic poetry, while two years later, it is supposed to be mythology. Perhaps, therefore, a few words of explanation are in order.

Athenäums-Fragment 116 ends with the assertion that "in a certain sense all poetry is or ought to be romantic," and a notebook jotting of 1797 states, "in a certain sense all poems are actually [*wohl*] *Romane*." [96] The expressions *romantische Poesie* and *Roman* would thus appear, in Schlegel's usage, to share the same connotations; yet while they overlap to a very large degree, they are not entirely synonymous. As we have seen, Shakespeare's plays could be referred to as *Romane*, but only by an extension of this word that strained its meaning to the limit. On the other hand, the term *Roman* denoted then among other things, as it does now almost exclusively, the modern, more or less realistic prose novel, which Schlegel did not consider to be romantic. In the "Brief über den Roman," an attempt is made at clearly distinguishing between the two terms. Having contrasted romantic poetry both with classical poetry and with the kind of literature (e.g., Lessing's *Emilia Galotti*) which is most certainly modern but quite unromantic, Schlegel explains that he considers Shakespeare to be the "actual center, the core of the romantic imagination," and continues:

This is where I seek and find the romantic, with the earlier moderns, with Shakespeare, Cervantes, in Italian poetry, in that age of knights, love, and fairy-tales, from which both the thing and the word itself are derived. This is the only thing till now that can form a contrast to the classical poems of antiquity; only these eternally fresh blossoms of the imagination are worthy of garlanding the ancient images of the gods. And it is certain that everything of the greatest excellence in modern poetry tends towards the romantic in its spirit and even in its genre [*Art*]—unless indeed it be a return to the ancient. Just as our poetry commenced with, and dissolved in, the *Roman*, so did that of the Greeks with and in the epic. Only with this difference, that the romantic is not a genre, but rather an element of poetry, which may predominate or recede to a greater or lesser extent, but which must never be wholly absent. It must thus be evident . . . that and why I demand that all poetry should be romantic, but abhor the *Roman* insofar as it aims at being a specific genre.[97]

It need hardly be pointed out that all of this is by now quite familiar to us; Schlegel had already told us that romantic poetry is "more than a genre" and "constitutes, as it were, poetry itself";[98] and he now merely repeats once again that his advocacy of romantic poetry excludes the *Roman* as a specific genre, i.e., the kind of modern prose novel that lacks both arabesque form and "sentimental" content and that was the staple trade of the lending libraries—the contemporary equivalent of the TV soap opera.

But if the expression *Roman* is neither to denote the modern prose novel nor to constitute an exact synonym for "romantic poetry," does it have any definable meaning left? Schlegel raises this question only to answer it by providing a rather odd definition: "A *Roman* is a romantic book." If this sounds like a tautology, he is quick to point out that it is not: the *Roman* is a *book* in the full sense of the word, intended to be read, in contrast to the stage-play. The latter should also be romantic, but is merely "an applied *Roman*."[99] Moreover, having the wide scope of a book rather than the limited extent of a stage-play, the *Roman* can be an independent, comprehensive whole; it can—though this time Schlegel avoids the term—aspire to the status of "universal poetry." We have once again come full circle and are back with *Athenäums-Fragment 116.*

CHAPTER 4

Lucinde

IN the winter and spring of 1798/99—about halfway between the writing of the "Athenäums-Fragmente" and the "Brief über den Roman," in both of which the theory of the novel plays such an important part—Schlegel also tried his hand as a practical novelist.

About one month after his arrival in Berlin, he had met the woman with whom he was to share the rest of his life: Dorothea Veit, the eldest daughter of Moses Mendelssohn. Dorothea, who was seven years older than Friedrich, had been married at the age of eighteen to one Simon Veit, a Berlin banker of immaculate character, though of rather limited intellectual interests. The marriage had not been a love match, but had been arranged by Dorothea's father, according to the custom of the times. By the time Schlegel arrived on the scene, Dorothea had lived with Veit for fourteen years, and there were two sons, Johannes and Philipp, who were subsequently to make a name for themselves as painters. But the marriage had long turned out a failure, and Friedrich, who was at the height of his intellectual powers and had not yet lost his good looks, promptly swept Dorothea off her feet. While she was certainly not beautiful, she, in turn, offered Friedrich the very thing for which, consciously or unconsciously, he had long been searching: the kind of relationship which combines friendship, intellectual empathy, and physical passion—the essential ingredients, as he believed, in marked contrast to the view then prevalent, of any relationship worthy to be hallowed with the name of love. In December, 1798, Dorothea left Veit; shortly afterward she obtained her divorce. In the following summer, Schlegel published the book that rendered his liaison with her notorious—the first and only part of his novel, *Lucinde*.[1]

Like Dorothea's marriage with Simon Veit, most middle- and upper-class marriages concluded in eighteenth-century Germany owed their existence largely to considerations of social status, money, or convenience. In fact, it was frequently argued that marriages ought to be based on reason rather than love: as love between husband and wife, it was thought, could not possibly last, its presence at the beginning would merely lead to subsequent disappointment. Sexual intercourse was widely held to be degrading, at least to women, and a double standard of morality was prevalent in practice, if not always in theory. To judge from French novels and plays of the eighteenth century, a man had to maintain relations with no less than three women to find full satisfaction: he needed a wife, who would be his loyal servant at home and bear his children, a mistress, who would provide physical satisfaction, and an *âme sœur*, whom he could place on a pedestal. It is a reflection of such views that Jacobi's Woldemar does not marry Henriette, whom he admires so much: "Anyone who has ever been in love," Jacobi explained to a friend, "knows that the first condition of love is animosity towards animal instincts." [2]

Schlegel's *Lucinde* is a passionate protest against the inequality of the sexes and the condemnation of sensuality. The mutual love of Julius and Lucinde celebrated in the novel—the former an obvious self-portrait, the latter a portrait of Dorothea—is *complete* love, both physical and spiritual. Such complete love, Schlegel held at that time, would in itself ensure faithfulness and thus constitute a marriage, rendering any religious and legal sanctions and ceremonies superfluous. (A marriage without love, Schlegel suggested in *Athenäums-Fragment 34,* is really only a concubinage; but even a marriage *à quatre,* if there was love, might be a real marriage.) Now, obviously, the kind of ideal relationship Schlegel wished to portray is, by its very nature, static; hence he found himself settled with the task of writing a novel without action. Fortunately, this was a problem with which his theory of the novel enabled him to deal.

After a brief "Prologue," in which Schlegel hints apologetically at his inability to provide the essential ingredient of verse, the novel begins with a letter written by Julius to Lucinde. As Julius explains, it had been his intention to tell in this letter the story of his apprenticeship as a lover. However, he is interrupted; and as he feels that nothing can serve his purpose better than to "destroy what we call order" in his composition and to "claim the right of charming confusion," he changes his plan and decides to inter-

pose, "entirely in the wrong place," a kind of essay he had written
for Lucinde on an earlier occasion, "Dithyrambic Fantasia on the
Most Beautiful Situation." This piece has something of the character of an overture in that it allows us a first glance at some of the
main *motifs* of the book: the predestination of lovers for each
other, death-in-love, the need to temper the consuming fire of love
with pleasantries, and, last but not least, the essential role love
plays in rounding off one's personality and making it complete
and harmonious. Until he met Lucinde, Julius avers, he would
never have thought it possible that one and the same woman
could be the "most tender sweetheart, the best companion and at
the same time a perfect friend." Such a complete relationship, Julius suggests, is only possible if the two partners in love do not
represent the prevalent ideals of extreme masculinity and feminin-
ity, but are both approaching a common ideal of perfect humanity. The "most beautiful situation"—that in which the lovers
change roles, the man imitating feminine passivity while the
woman assumes masculine impetuousness—is an allegory of this
state of perfection.

Now Julius has already hinted that his letter, though addressed
to Lucinde, is intended for publication; and hence he feels the
need to justify the "insolence" of wishing to *write* what one is
"hardly allowed to say." This justification is attempted in the next
section, a pen portrait of a three-year-old girl, who is still young
enough to be uninhibited and whose behavior—innocent though
it is—shows us that prudery is unnatural.

The fourth section, "Allegory of Insolence," deals with the same
topic in a more ambitious manner. It begins by illustrating the
folly of public opinion that forces women to display prudery and
continues by introducing to the puzzled reader four handsome
youths, who have to decide between allegorical representations of
Modesty, Propriety, Seemliness, and similar supposed virtues on
the one hand, and Insolence on the other. Reference to Schlegel's
private letters and the examination of his notebooks reveal that
the youths are personifications of *Lucinde* and three other novels
that Schlegel was planning to write, but also—as K. K. Polheim
has discovered—of four ideal types of *Roman*.[3] This rather silly
extravaganza is followed by some of the most brilliant pages of
the whole novel, in which the psychology of sex and the sexes is
discussed, and by speculations on the kind of reception that a

novel in which Insolence is preferred to Modesty is likely to have.

The fifth section, "Idyll Concerning Idleness," is an attack on a trait of his times which seemed to Schlegel no less inimical to the happiness of lovers than prudishness—the widespread idolization of "diligence and utility," which Julius compares to the "Angel of Death who prevents man from returning to Paradise." Schlegel's critics were quick to accuse him of advocating laziness; what he really intended was to safeguard, in the midst of a society given at the same time to utilitarianism and to the cult of work as an end in itself, the capacity for leisure, the "breath of life [*Lebensluft*] of innocence and enthusiasm."

The sixth section is a dialogue between Julius and Lucinde—an imitation in prose of a poem ascribed to Bion, in which a conversation between two lovers leads on to caresses and to physical union.[4] This section was probably intended to portray the synthesis of the spiritual and the sensual which Schlegel had so much at heart; but he himself subsequently realized that he had not done justice to his subject. The dialogue, clever though it is, does not ring true; there is none of the gradual unfolding of passion which the subject demands, and the conclusion of the chapter follows abruptly upon a discussion of jealousy that is surely placed in the wrong context.

The first six sections of *Lucinde* amount to exactly one third of the whole work. The second third is taken up by a continuous narrative, in which Julius, as he had intended to do at the beginning, recounts his education as a lover and thus substantiates his assertion that love alone can make one's personality complete and harmonious. Unfortunately, the narrative is so compressed as to be colorless; as Dorothea's sister put it, it is a *"Romanextrakt"* rather than a *"Roman."* [5] For our purposes, it will suffice to mention one single episode from this central section: Julius has a love affair with a prostitute, whose conduct suggests that a harlot may be more virtuous than many women who make a profession of displaying their virtue. This idea caught on, and noble harlots occur frequently in later Romantic novels. The narrative ends with Julius' discovery of Lucinde and a brief evocation of their happiness.

Preceded by six shorter pieces, the long narrative section is also followed by six shorter pieces. The imposition of such symmetry on a work in which, as its interposed author puts it, "charming confusion" prevails, gives the novel the "witty form" which Schlegel expected romantic poetry to have. The last third begins with a short symbolic representation of the "metamorphoses" which love brings about in Julius' character and in his outlook on life. Then there are two letters to Lucinde, constituting a single section, which at long last take us beyond the point in time at which the novel begins. Lucinde is pregnant, and Julius looks forward to the child. She falls ill, and Julius realizes how desolate his life would be without her. The letters are followed by a "Reflection" that deals with the topic of procreation and the omnipresence of sexual polarity in nature, but parodies at the same time the fashionable philosophical terminology of the day, particularly that of Fichte. At the end of this piece, Julius apologizes for the obscurity of the allusions and attempts to prepare the reader for the next piece, two letters to a friend with the title "Julius to Antonio." While these letters are, no doubt, intended to parallel those written to Lucinde, adding a discussion of friendship to that of love, they are poorly integrated in the novel and seem to owe their presence in it to the fact that Schlegel had a quarrel with Schleiermacher just when he was beginning to run out of ideas.

The penultimate section of the novel, "Yearning and Rest," a dialogue between Julius and Lucinde in poetic (predominantly iambic) prose, introduces an idea which Schlegel was the first among the Romantics to express in print. In spite of the happiness they enjoy in each others' arms, the lovers yearn for death, for the eternal night that would render their union still more perfect, shelter it from the demands of reality, and protect it from the ravages of time. Subsequently, the *motif* became fashionable among the Romantics and, long after the decline of the Romantic movement, found its most poignant expression in the second act of Wagner's *Tristan*.[6]

After "Yearning and Rest," Schlegel was left with a final problem of considerable difficulty—that of finding a suitable conclusion for a novel that had virtually no action. He solved the problem ingeniously: the last piece, "Triflings of the Imagination," is written in a prose that becomes more and more transparent, producing the effect of a pianissimo that finally merges into silence.

The connections between Schlegel's novel and his poetic theory are so obvious that they need not be labored. The novel aims at "universality" by combining a wide variety of genres—the letter, the dithyrambic fantasia, allegory, idyl, parody, and straight narrative. It represents an attempt at fusing and intermingling art and criticism, poetry and philosophy, and—if only to a limited extent—the epic, dramatic, and lyric genres: there is straight "epic" narrative, extended "dramatic" dialogue and, as we have seen, a section in poetic prose—a substitute for the lyrical poetry which Schlegel, as he apologetically points out in the "Prologue," was unable to write.

Most strikingly, the novel exploits the technique of the interposed narrator in such a way as to display the fusion of enthusiasm, caprice, self-criticism, and deliberate structuring demanded by Schlegel's theory; *Lucinde* is an obvious illustration of the "witty" or "arabesque" form that Schlegel had singled out as a distinguishing feature of romantic poetry. On the other hand, Schlegel's theory of poetry certainly called for far more imaginative and less earth-bound and realistic works than his own novel, and the connection between *Lucinde* and the romantic tradition he wished to revive is tenuous indeed. Schlegel did himself a disservice by mentioning Boccaccio, Petrarch, and Dante in the prologue of the novel, thereby inviting comparisons that could not conceivably be to his advantage. He was, after all, a critic rather than a poet, and lacked the very talents a novelist can least do without: the ability to create living, convincing characters, a truly fertile imagination, and the evocative power that makes the reader visualize and emotionally respond to what he is told. But the little work—it amounts to about 30,000 words—is nonetheless, if not a success, at least a very distinguished failure. The view of sex and the sexes presented in it is of a refreshing sanity that was very rare indeed in its own day. It is one of the earliest experimental novels in European letters and anticipates techniques that were fully exploited only in the twentieth century.

Contrary to its reputation, *Lucinde* is not a pornographic novel, not even by the standards of its own time. In fact, Schlegel, who so much enjoyed provoking his readers in other works, occasionally pulled his punches in *Lucinde*. Thus, to take a random example, it is from his private notebooks rather than from his novel that we learn of his conviction that, a wedding being an "ugly sacrifice," girls "ought to be seduced." [7] Or, again, where the notebook plainly tells us that "he who cannot satisfy a woman is impotent," that "most men are impotent" in this sense, that "impotence invalidates the marriage" and that, consequently, "adultery is far rarer than people think," the corresponding passage in the novel is couched in such vague terms that most readers probably miss the point.[8]

If the publication of *Lucinde* nonetheless caused a scandal and made its author so notorious that ten years later one still wondered in the *salons* of Budapest whether it was proper to introduce Schlegel to the ladies, this is only partly due to the contents of the novel itself. Rather, the many enemies he and his brother had made by their literary criticism found in *Lucinde* a magnificent opportunity for revenge: while around 1800 there was no dearth of authors who—by the standards of his critics—led far more dissolute lives than Schlegel, and no dearth of books that—by the same standards—presented far more dissolute views, Schlegel had committed the unforgivable crime of living what he preached. Goethe had a mistress, but refrained from advocating this practice; Wilhelm Heinse glorified promiscuity (which was not at all what Schlegel had advocated), but did so in a book that could not very easily be read as a *roman-à-clef*. Schlegel both had a mistress and wrote about it frankly and without apologies—and was made to pay dearly for this mistake.

Presumably because of the scandal caused by its first publication, *Lucinde* was not reissued during Schlegel's lifetime. It was rescued from oblivion in the 1830's by writers such as Gutzkow, who quite erroneously saw in it a confirmation of their own doctrines of free love; and it has since been reprinted time and again. Two paperback series—*Reclam's Universalbibliothek* (1870ff.) and the *Insel-Bücherei* (1920)—made the book readily available, and there can be no doubt that, with all its defects, *Lucinde* is the most widely read German Romantic novel.

CHAPTER 5

Years of Transition

I *The Jena Circle*

ON September 1, 1799, Schlegel left Berlin and joined his brother in Jena. In October, Dorothea followed him, and for the next two years, the house of Wilhelm and Caroline became the meeting place of the whole movement. Schelling, who lectured at the University of Jena, was the most frequent visitor, while Novalis often came from nearby Weissenfels. Tieck paid visits from Berlin and lived in Jena from October, 1799, to the following July. At times, Caroline had more than a dozen dinner guests to provide for, and the social gatherings in her house have become legendary for their gaiety and wit.

Schelling and such relatively minor figures as Steffens, Ritter, and Hülsen were at work on the strange amalgam of science, deductive philosophy, and untrammeled speculation which, as Friedrich Schlegel hoped, would give rise to a new mythology. Tieck and Novalis became close friends and saw to it that Christianity was, as Dorothea put it, "à l'ordre du jour."[1] Friedrich Schlegel taught Dorothea, Caroline, and Schelling Italian; and both brothers devoted many evenings to the study of Dante. In October, 1799, they paid daily visits to Goethe, who had come to Jena from Weimar. A. W. Schlegel and Tieck were past masters of the art of parody and rivaled each other in brilliant sallies against their common literary enemies. The whole circle joined in reading Schiller's deeply serious "Lied von der Glocke" and laughed so much that they almost fell off their chairs. "Such an eternal concert of wit, poetry, art, and science as surrounds me here," Dorothea wrote back to Berlin, "can easily make one forget the rest of the world."[2]

The group was at the height of its productivity. Novalis wrote his *Hymnen an die Nacht* and the first and only part of his novel, *Heinrich von Ofterdingen*. His essay, *Die Christenheit oder Europa* (1799), remained unpublished till 1826, but greatly impressed his friends and helped to establish the trend of the movement toward Catholicism and the cult of the Middle Ages. Tieck reinforced this trend with the dramatic poem *Genoveva*, published in his *Romantische Dichtungen* (2 vols., 1799–1800). Schelling wrote his *System des transzendentalen Idealismus* (1800–1803). A. W. Schlegel published German versions of sixteen of Shakespeare's plays between 1797 and 1801, thus establishing himself as Germany's most accomplished translator; he continued his activities as a critic and lyrical poet and also found the time to write a play, *Ion* (1801).

The Romantics—though, to be sure, they did not refer to themselves as such—began to make disciples, such as Clemens Brentano, who for a while attached himself to Friedrich and Dorothea. The latter had no personal ambitions as a writer, but put pen to paper so as to help Friedrich earn a living and scored a minor success with her novel, *Florentin* (1801). Thus, one can hardly blame the Schlegels and their friends if they became a little intoxicated with their own achievements and felt that the new science, the new philosophy, and their own poetry were about to usher in a new age. But their moment of triumph was short-lived.

Friedrich Schlegel, who had provided intellectual leadership for the group and given it a sense of direction, was approaching a crisis. It had cost him a tremendous effort to complete the "Gespräch über die Poesie," and he was beginning to spend far more time on amassing notes toward projects than on bringing these projects to a successful conclusion. Also, he was venturing into new fields, for the time being with disastrous results. From October, 1800, to March, 1801, he lectured at the University of Jena on Transcendental Philosophy. These lectures were attended by Hegel, who seems to be indebted to them for a starting point in the development of his dialectics;[3] but they attracted far fewer students than Schlegel had hoped and were generally judged as being poorly prepared and difficult to follow.

Moreover, Schlegel had learned the art of versification from his brother and from Tieck,[4] and henceforth regarded himself as a poet, with the result that he produced, during the rest of his life, some four hundred pages of inferior verse and spent untold hours planning numerous plays, epics, romances and novels—among them a second, third, and even a fourth part of *Lucinde*—that, mercifully, remained unwritten. The one play he did complete,

Alarcos (1802), is not entirely devoid of historical interest. It is an early product of the German Romantics' discovery of Calderón, whom Schlegel imitated in his choice of a Christian subject matter and in the use of a profuse variety of Romance verse forms—rhymed and assonant hendecasyllabics, terza rima, quintillas, octavas, silvas, stanzas, and sonnets. The use of trimeters and the role assigned to fate in the play suggest that Schlegel aimed at combining classical with the far more obvious romantic traits of the work and thus to make it an example of the synthesis of the ancient and the modern that he never ceased to dream of. "The purpose of *Alarcos*," he wrote in retrospect, "must be clear to everybody: it is intended to be a tragedy, in the ancient sense of the word, but with a romantic subject and form." [5]

In spite of such high ambitions, *Alarcos* is, however, the poorest work Schlegel ever produced, ill-conceived in its plot and bombastic in its execution. Largely in order to train his actors in speaking verse, Goethe—against Schiller's advice—produced the play in Weimar, but the public soon became restless and, at a critical moment of the play, burst into laughter. Goethe, asserting his immense personal authority, commanded silence, and the performance concluded "without the least sign of approval" on the part of the audience. It is interesting to note, however, that when the performance was repeated in Bad Lauchstädt, the students of the nearby University of Halle, who frequented the summer theater at Lauchstädt, either genuinely approved of the play or at least, as Karl von Raumer reports, considered it their duty to defend Schlegel against his opponents. The battle between the new and the old school was in full swing, and among the younger generation the Romantic taste was in the ascendant. [6]

A more successful venture than *Alarcos* was Schlegel's publication, jointly with his brother, of two volumes of critical essays and reviews, *Charakteristiken und Kritiken* (1801). In this collection, Schlegel reprinted, with minor changes, his reviews of *Woldemar,* of *Wilhelm Meisters Lehrjahre,* and of Niethammer's *Philosophisches Journal,* as well as his studies of Forster and Lessing. The latter study, as it will be remembered, was a fragment. In the winter of 1800/1801, Schlegel was still at a loss how to continue, and finally wrote a conclusion that had little to do with what went before and dealt more with himself than with Lessing. The second volume of the *Charakteristiken und Kritiken* contained, however, an entirely new essay by him, a study of Boccaccio,[7] in which he made significant contributions to the theory of a genre that is vastly more important in German than in English literature—the *novella*.[8]

Charakteristiken und Kritiken marks the end of Friedrich's and Wilhelm's years of collaboration. The Jena circle was falling apart. In the fall of 1800, the *Athenäum*, which had not been selling well, ceased publication. Tieck had moved to Dresden; Novalis died in March, 1801; and Schlegel, for various reasons, quarreled with most of his friends. Before leaving Berlin, he had signed a publisher's contract for a translation of Plato's works, to be done in collaboration with Schleiermacher. Subsequently, he defaulted on his share of the undertaking; and the theologian, who was meticulous in carrying out obligations, performed the whole enormous task on his own, ceased to consult his dilatory friend, and mutual recriminations led to a gradual estrangement. In the meantime, Schlegel had interfered in a love affair between Brentano and Sophie Mereau. In 1803 Brentano discovered what had happened and turned from a disciple into an enemy. Worst of all, the friendship between Schlegel and his brother suffered a blow from which it never completely recovered. During the first few weeks after Dorothea's move to Jena, she got on very well with Caroline, but sharing the latter's house inevitably led to friction. Also, Friedrich and Dorothea discovered that Caroline and Schelling had fallen in love, and while Wilhelm was prepared to grant her a divorce and remain friends with her, Friedrich was hurt that his sister-in-law should prefer someone else—and a rival philosopher at that!—to his admired brother. Realizing that she had Friedrich and Dorothea against her, Caroline set out to stir up trouble between them and her husband, succeeding all the more easily as Wilhelm spent the summer of 1800 with Schelling in Bamberg.

In February, 1801, Wilhelm moved to Berlin, where, in the next three years, he delivered his famous lectures on esthetics and poetry, *Über schöne Literatur und Kunst*. Though these lectures were not published until 1884, they were very influential when they were given and spread the gospel of Romanticism far and wide. Wilhelm drew heavily on Friedrich, but modified his ideas sufficiently to render them less paradoxical and extreme, and hence more readily acceptable. While Friedrich, with his uncompromising devotion to saying things as he saw them, saying them in his own way, and not shirking any difficulties, had only too often drowned, as it were, in his own depth and become incomprehensible, Wilhelm, who prized clarity, turned out to be an excellent popularizer and harvested, in terms of public acclaim, what his brother had so laboriously sown. When Wilhelm left Germany in 1804 to accompany Madame de Staël to Coppet and on her travels, it was he rather than Friedrich who was generally considered the founder of the Romantic doctrine.

By the summer of 1801, Friedrich and Dorothea, who had remained in Jena, found themselves in almost complete isolation and in severe financial straits. Uncertain where to turn or what to do next, Friedrich left Jena in December, spent six weeks in Berlin, and then moved to Dresden, where Dorothea joined him. On February 15, he wrote back to Berlin, under the seal of secrecy, that he had decided to move to Paris, where he hoped to find other means of supporting himself than by writing; for, as he explained, it had become "more and more unbearable" to him to live by his pen.[9] Even so, he stayed in Dresden till May and then visited Leipzig, where he found a publisher for a new periodical, *Europa,* to be edited from Paris. Passing through Weimar in time to witness the failure of his play, he arrived in the French capital toward the end of June.

As we shall see, Paris brought Schlegel new friends, new inspirations, and new fields of activity. Even so, one cannot but regard his leaving Germany with a tinge of regret. Henceforth—whether in Paris, Cologne, or Vienna—Schlegel was at the periphery of German literary life rather than at its center, and was no longer a sufficiently close, sufficiently involved eyewitness. The literary developments were, however, influenced by him to a far greater extent than scholarship has demonstrated as yet. The influence is most obvious in the field of literary theory. It was because of *Athenäums-Fragment 116* and the "Gespräch über die Poesie" that the word *romantisch* caught on in the special sense in which it was contrasted with *klassisch* and that the writing of essays, treatises, and even poems contrasting the classical with the romantic became fashionable. In due course, as more and more of the younger poets and writers developed along lines foreshadowed, if not preempted, by the Schlegels, Novalis, and Tieck, cultivating complicated Romance verse forms, exhibiting a preference for

Catholic and medieval subjects, and—though, oddly enough, to Schlegel's annoyance—paying increasing attention to folk songs and popular ballads, their classicistic enemies dubbed the whole new school romantic, using the word once again as a term of abuse. After a period of complete semantic confusion, this new meaning, now cleansed of its pejorative connotations, became dominant, and from the 1830's onward, the terms *Romantik, Romantiker,* and *romantische Poesie* began to refer primarily to the literary movement that dominated the first third of the nineteenth century, to its protagonists, and their writings.

But Schlegel's influence was, of course, by no means confined to matters of terminology. No one turning from a study of the Schlegels to Jean Paul's *Vorschule der Aesthetik* (1804), to the critical writings published in the *avant-garde* periodicals between 1800 and 1830, or to the theoretical utterances of the great majority of the younger poets whom we now call Romantic can fail to be struck by the breadth and depth of the influence of the two brothers. As regards practice rather than theory, there are many works —Brentano's *Godwi,* Tieck's *Oktavian,* Hoffmann's *Kater Murr,* to name three obvious examples—which illustrate most strikingly what Schlegel meant by such terms as "universal poetry" and "arabesque form"; though the task of ascertaining to what extent this was due to the novels of Jean Paul (some of which predate the *Athenäum*), to Schlegel's theories, and to various intermediaries, would be an arduous task indeed. But Schlegel himself watched most of these developments with a jaundiced eye: it is not the least among the many oddities of his life that in his later years this great pioneer of Romanticism showed so little enthusiasm for most of the works that bear the imprint of his thought and which we now—thanks to him—call Romantic.

II *The Periodical* Europa

The two years Schlegel spent in Paris present a puzzle to his biographer. His Paris notebooks are crowded with titles of plays, novels, and romances he was planning to write—dozens of titles, which he kept changing and rearranging, grouping and regrouping in patterns of four, eight, and sixteen. On reading these pages with their countless repetitions and contradictions, one gets the impression of a mind obsessed. Yet in other ways, these years were extremely productive.

While the *Athenäum* had been a biannual publication, his new periodical, *Europa,* was planned, more ambitiously, as a quarterly.[10] Schlegel had counted on substantial contributions from his friends in Germany, but was soon short of copy, and by the time the fourth and last issue of *Europa* appeared, eighteen months later than planned, he had had to write a full third of the periodical himself.

Europa opens with an account of Friedrich's journey to Paris, "Reise nach Frankreich," which vividly illustrates the extent to which the extravagant hopes for a better future that he had entertained around 1799 had been dashed. Leaving Germany had aroused his patriotism, but the two poems he wrote on the occasion celebrate the past rather than the present and are accompanied by sad reflections on "what the Germans had been once" (in the Middle Ages), "what they could be," and what they were now.[11] The rather superficial characterization of the French that follows gives them credit for gaiety, *esprit,* and scientific ability, but denies them all talent for music, poetry, and painting.

The rest of the essay strikes a note of mysticism that reflects Schlegel's study of Böhme, to whose writings Tieck had introduced him. Europe, we are told, does not have the unity commonly ascribed to it, but is rent by a dichotomy of North and South. Such dichotomies are a characteristic feature of the European civilization, which has been vitiated, from its beginnings, by an unnatural separation of Poetry and Philosophy (i.e., of man's imaginative and his reasoning powers). This separation is responsible for the Europeans' "total incapacity for religion" and the "complete atrophy" of their "higher faculties."[12] In modern Europe, man has sunk to his lowest depths—a fact from which it does *not* follow that he must soon rise again. On the contrary: if Europe is to see better times, its broken spirit must be restored by the healing influence of Asia, particularly India, where the faculties of the human mind have remained integrated and which is therefore the home and eternal source of religion. The East (Asia) and the North (Northern Europe) are the "visible poles of the Good Principle" on earth.[13]

It can hardly be claimed that these speculations formed an auspicious beginning for Schlegel's new journalistic venture. His second contribution to his periodical, an essay with the title "Literatur" and largely devoted to pressing the claims of philosophic

Idealism, was equally unlikely to gain him new friends. Idealism is said to be "the center and the basis of German literature; no physics comprehending the whole of nature is possible without it, and higher poetry, being a different expression of the same transcendental view, differs from Idealism only in its form." [14] The essay provides an attractive and interesting summary of the activities of the Romantic circle, but was bound to strike Schlegel's readers as one-sided and written in the interest of his own faction.

Schlegel's last contribution to the first issue of *Europa* was a description of paintings in the Louvre—the first of a series of five articles on this form of art.[15] It is this series that represents the main achievement of Schlegel's periodical.

In the absence of techniques for a reasonably accurate reproduction of paintings, descriptions were the only means available at that time for acquainting art lovers abroad with the collections in Paris, which had been recently enriched by numerous paintings sent home by the French armies from their campaigns in Italy and the Low Countries. Schlegel thus had the incentive, but also the handicap of writing about works of art for a public that was denied all direct experience of them. In response to this task, he developed considerable descriptive powers, but inevitably tended to emphasize what he called the "poetry" or the "spirit" of the paintings rather than their form.

No doubt, such a method is open to the objection that it pays least attention to those features of paintings that give them their characteristic pictorial value; it would, for instance, be totally incapable of dealing with abstract art. But this is an objection Schlegel would not have entertained. In his view, it was the function of painting to "glorify religion and to reveal its mysteries even more beautifully and clearly than can be done in words," so that the value of a painting lay not in its sensuous qualities, nor in its "charm and beauty," but in its symbolic meaning, in the signification of the divine, without which a picture "does not deserve to be called a work of art." [16]

To a certain extent, of course, this had already been said by Wackenroder; but Schlegel was more consistent, and hence more radical, in his conclusions. Wackenroder still felt—like the classicists—that the high Renaissance represented the supreme achievement in European painting (though, of course, he did not use the *term* "Renaissance" and thought of this period as belonging to the Middle Ages). Schlegel's scale of values was different. According to him, it had been the early Italian painters who had been most loyal to the true, religious function of art. The young Raphael, who was still inspired by loving piety, had risen to the greatest height; subsequently, misled by the splendors of antiquity and by the example of Michelangelo, he had strayed from the "pious path of love." With Raphael, Michelangelo, Titian, Correggio, and Giulio Romano, the "decay of art" had begun; Titian, Correggio, and their contemporaries were the "last painters" worthy of that name.[17]

Linked with early Italian painting in Schlegel's mind was what he called the "old German school" of Van Eyck, Dürer, and Holbein, as well as such painters as Altdorfer and Memling, who were then almost completely unknown. Here, as in so many other ways, Schlegel's writings on art must be seen in relation to their own day, if their importance is to be realized. French and German painting, art criticism, and art instruction were dominated by classicism: Art students were supposed to learn painting from the study of plaster casts of Greek and Roman sculptures and to demonstrate what they had learned in this way by painting scenes from the Homeric epics. No less a figure than Goethe supported these sterile and misguided practices with all his energy and authority. Thus, Schlegel's new doctrines, one-sided as they may seem to *us*, had a wholesome and liberating influence. Goethe was furious, and it was Schlegel's new theory of art, not of poetry, that put an end to the tacit alliance that had so long existed between the great poet and the Romantics. But the young generation thrilled to the new teachings, and Schlegel had the satisfaction of seeing his and Wackenroder's theories put into practice by a whole group of painters, the *Lucasbund,* which included such artists as Overbeck, Pforr, Cornelius, Schadow, and Schlegel's stepsons Johannes and Philipp Veit.[18]

III   *The Paris Lectures on Literature*

While the first three issues of *Europa* had appeared, reasonably promptly, in 1803, the fourth and last was delayed till 1805; first the publisher and then Schlegel himself had lost interest in the quarterly, which sold badly and so proved a poor investment. Schlegel's attempts at finding suitable employment—among other things, he had dreamed of founding an Academy of German

Writers in Paris—also failed. He now produced a Lessing anthology in three volumes, to which he himself contributed five essays. But though a good deal of thought had gone into this publication —Schlegel's selection of extracts from Lessing's writings is stimulating, and his own contributions would merit detailed discussion in a longer book—it did not catch on, and a substantial part of the first and only printing was still unsold six years later. Thus, Schlegel would have been in dire straits indeed if he had not been helped out by a fortunate accident. In the fall of 1803, the sons of a wealthy German businessman, Sulpiz and Melchior Boisserée, were touring France, accompanied by a friend, J. B. Bertram. Having been appreciative readers of *Europa*, the three travelers called on Schlegel, and their visit had important results: the Boisserées and their friend decided to stay in Paris as Dorothea's paying guests and engaged Friedrich to lecture to them on European literature.[19]

The text of these lectures has been preserved and shows that Schlegel's views on European literature had undergone no fundamental change since 1800; in fact, the most informative passage on the *Roman* and on romantic poetry reads, in part at least, like a paraphrase of *Athenäums-Fragment 116:*

> The concept of the *Roman* as established by Boccaccio and Cervantes is that of a *romantic book,* a romantic composition in which all forms and genres are mingled and intertwined . . . There are historical, rhetorical and dialogic passages; all these styles . . . are mixed and combined with one another in the most significant and artful ways. Poetry of every kind,—lyrical, epic, didactic poetry and romances (*Romanzen*)—are scattered throughout the whole work . . . The *Roman* is a poem consisting of poems, a whole tissue of poems . . . Such a poetic composition . . . makes possible a much more artful poetic structure (*Verschlingung von Poesie*) than the epic or the drama, in which at least unity of tone prevails. . . . Here, where the poet may entirely abandon himself to his fanciful caprice, the outpourings of his own moods, his playful humor, where no unity of tone prevents his being serious and jesting in turn, monotony is almost impossible. The *Roman* is the most original, the most characteristic, and the most perfect form of romantic poetry . . .[20]

There are, however, changes in detail. Since 1800, Schlegel had added Calderón and Camoens to his canon of great romantic poets and had studied the Provençal manuscripts which—as yet undiscovered by the French—gathered dust in the *Bibliothèque Nationale*. Above all, there is nothing in these lectures that corresponds to the theories of the "Rede über die Mythologie." The religious convictions that form the background to these lectures are Christian rather than pantheistic.

IV *Cologne, 1804–1808*

As the Boisserées, who now provided Schlegel with his only reliable source of income, never intended to stay in France for more than a few months, his days in Paris were numbered. On April 6, 1804, he legalized his relations with Dorothea. Their union was solemnized by the same pastor who, eighteen years previously, had married Germaine Necker to Eric de Staël-Holstein. On April 11, Schlegel gave his last lecture, and toward the end of the month, he accompanied his friends on a walking tour through France and Belgium to Cologne, where he was to spend the next four years.

Guided by the Boisserées, Schlegel had developed a taste for medieval architecture, which at that time was still commonly regarded as ill-proportioned and barbarous. His journey to Cologne, which soon turned into a pilgrimage from one medieval building to another, and a second journey to Paris, undertaken in the following winter, form the subject of a series of "Letters"—"Briefe auf einer Reise durch die Niederlande, Rheingegenden, die Schweiz und einen Teil von Frankreich" [21]—which, published in 1805, constitute the most significant landmark in the rediscovery of the Gothic style in Germany. Unaware of the French origin of Gothic architecture, which was only demonstrated in 1840 by Franz Mertens, Schlegel considered this style to be "uniquely appropriate" to Germany; his "Letters" thus occasionally display a patriotism unwarranted by the facts. They are, however, a pioneering venture of major significance. As W. D. Robson-Scott has shown, the "Letters" were "the first publication of any length in German literature to deal predominantly with the subject of medieval architecture," and the first publication to point out the significant part played by sculpture in the Gothic system. It was through this work that "the Gothic revival became firmly anchored as a constituent part of the German Romantic movement." Schlegel was the first who fully appreciated the splendor of Gothic glass windows, and while he used the term "Gothic" to cover the whole of medieval architecture, he made the first serious attempt to distinguish between the two styles that we now call Gothic and Romanesque.[22]

Soon after their arrival in Cologne, the brothers Boisserée began to buy up paintings threatened with destruction by the secularization—under the *Code Napoléon*—of churches and monasteries, and thus laid the foundations of their famous art collection. They also attended lecture courses on literature, philosophy, and history given by Schlegel partly for them alone and partly for a somewhat larger circle organized by them; and they did their best to keep their promise of finding him a position appropriate to his fame and learning. Contrary to expectations, however, the University of Cologne, which had been closed by the French in 1798, was not reopened; and when Schlegel applied for a professorship at Würzburg, Schelling was his sole supporter in the faculty. For a while, in return for a pittance, he taught school, and occasionally, through the good offices of his brother, he was helped out by Mme de Staël, but he was never very far from destitution. Despair now threatened to sap his productivity as a writer, and it took him till December, 1807, to complete the work, first planned in 1805, on which his dwindling hopes for a professorship now depended: the treatise *Über die Sprache und Weisheit der Indier.*

V *The Language and Wisdom of India*

Among Westerners, the study of Sanskrit had been pioneered by missionaries, mainly Jesuits, one of whom, J. E. Hanxleden (1681–1732), was the first European to publish a Sanskrit grammar, while another, Gaston Cœurdoux, showed in 1767 that Sanskrit, Greek, and Latin had common roots. Voltaire, and subsequently Herder, had repeatedly referred to India as the cradle of mankind; and from about 1785 on, an increasing number of translations from Sanskrit originals became available, largely as a result of the pioneering efforts of Charles Wilkins and William Jones. Friedrich Schlegel, as will be remembered, had a brother who died in India; subsequently, his interest in India was stimulated by Herder and finally by Friedrich Majer, whom he met in Jena in 1800, and who in 1801 pointed out similarities between Indic theology and German philosophic Idealism.

From 1799, Schlegel himself had repeatedly referred to India or, more vaguely, to the "Orient" as a possible source of inspiration, but had based his remarks on hearsay rather than on genuine knowledge. Soon after his arrival in Paris, however, his curiosity had been aroused by the wealth of oriental manuscripts in the *Bibliothèque Nationale*. In the winter of 1802/1803, he studied Persian and made plans to write a Persian grammar, but abandoned this project when a stroke of luck enabled him to pursue a far more exciting venture. He met Alexander Hamilton, the only person on the Continent who knew Sanskrit. Hamilton, a British naval officer who had recently returned from India and had been surprised in Paris by the resumption of hostilities between England and France after the Peace of Amiens, was now a prisoner of war on parole and could well spare the time to instruct Schlegel for no other reward than that of having so gifted a pupil. Schlegel approached his new field with boundless enthusiasm, convinced that he was at the fountainhead of all human wisdom. "Here is the actual source of all languages, of all thoughts and poems of the human spirit," he wrote to Tieck on September 15, 1803; "*everything*, everything originates from India without exception." [23]

Subsequently, his ardor somewhat diminished—not so much, as has been suggested, because Indian life and letters fell short of the mythical image Schlegel had formed,[24] but for a more personal reason. When he began to learn Sanskrit, he felt that Europe's only hope for a religious renaissance lay in drawing inspirations from the remote East. By the time he had acquired some mastery of the language, he had reached the conviction that Christianity was not one mythology among many, but the Truth, and hence no such elevated role could be assigned to India. Schlegel's famous treatise *Über die Sprache und Weisheit der Indier*, published in 1808, was thus a very different book from anything he might have written three or four years previously; but it proved a milestone in the history of scholarship nonetheless.

The treatise begins with an account of the Sanskrit language, whose relation to other Indo-European languages is pointed out. This had been done before, but Schlegel was the first to insist clearly and decisively on the importance of grammatical structure, rather than vocabulary, in comparing languages and determining their relationship.[25] It was in this connection that Schlegel promoted the term "comparative grammar"—coined by his brother[26] —which plays such an important part in modern philology. His conviction that the other Indo-European languages had de-

scended from Sanskrit was, of course, erroneous, but his attempts
to substantiate this belief contributed appreciably to the discovery
that Sanskrit was closest to the hypothetical origin of the whole
family of languages and to the development of more refined
methods of philological investigation in general. The discussion of
various types of grammatical structures in this section of Schlegel's treatise prepared the ground for the famous distinction between "synthetic" and "analytic" languages subsequently formulated by his brother.

The second section of Schlegel's treatise presents a survey of
Indic philosophy and affords us a first glimpse of the view of history that he was now beginning to adopt. Sharing the widespread
error that the Pentateuch chronologically preceded the earliest
Indic theologies, Schlegel was persuaded that the history of religious beliefs only made sense on the assumption of an original
revelation, which had subsequently been "misunderstood" and
corrupted, this giving rise to such aberrations as pantheism and
polytheism. Thus, he asserted, it was in the *earliest* Sanskrit traditions that the "purest concepts of the Godhead" were to be found,
though even then they were already tainted with superstitions.[27]
In the third section of the treatise, which is devoted to "Ideas on
History," the degradation theory of religion, which had been proposed previously, e.g., by Joseph Butler in England, is matched
by a corresponding theory of the development of mankind. At
least some races, it is here asserted, had not originated in a state of
"animal stupor," but in one of high perfection—the perfection
preceding man's "apostasy from God"—and their subsequent history had in the main been one of decline. Thus, Schlegel replaced
his earlier, optimistic view of perpetual progress by a historical
pessimism tempered only by his religious beliefs.

Arguing both from the traces of the original revelation which he
claimed to have discerned in the earliest Sanskrit writings and
from the grammatical complexity of Sanskrit, which he considered
to be superior to less ancient, grammatically simpler languages,
Schlegel particularly emphasized the noble beginnings of the Indians, who are consequently credited with a somewhat extravagant role in the history of civilization. Schlegel correctly ac-
counted for the spread of what we now call the Indo-European
languages by the migrations of peoples speaking these languages
—migrations which he somewhat quaintly ascribed not only to

such natural causes as overpopulation, but also to the "fear and dissolute greed" resulting from man's apostasy from God. He quite erroneously concluded, however, that the world's "greatest empires and noblest nations"—including, among others, ancient Egypt, Mexico and Peru—all owed their origins to Indian colonization. Thus, prompted by the noblest motives, Schlegel planted the seeds of that pernicious theory according to which all civilizations spring from the activities of a single, "Aryan" race.[28]

Schlegel's treatise is rounded off by some eighty pages of translations of Sanskrit poetry. The knowledge of Sanskrit displayed by this section of the book is by no means that of a modern expert, but is highly creditable for a pioneer of the language.[29] Schlegel's German renderings, however, are so stiff and awkward as to be almost unreadable. Altogether, virtually every statement one can make about the book has to be qualified. An odd mixture of objective scholarship and subjective philosophizing, of facts, intuitions, brilliant insights, and reckless speculations, *Über die Sprache und Weisheit der Indier* was both a major success and a minor failure. Schlegel's recently gained and still somewhat confused Catholic convictions time and again intrude upon his scholarly arguments and give large sections of the book a factional and partisan atmosphere. As a result, his new publication made him new enemies, both among those who considered any expression of Catholic sympathies a crime against reason and among those who were annoyed by his attacks on pantheism; the very book which Schlegel hoped would procure him a professorship made it less likely that he should get one. Yet in other ways his treatise on India magnificently achieved its purpose. It was as a direct result of this treatise that the two great founders of Sanskrit philology as an academic discipline, A. W. Schlegel and Franz Bopp, took up Indic studies, and that India, which had so long been a mere "mythical image," [30] at long last became an object of scholarly study in Germany. Besides, Schlegel's attacks on pantheism not only caused annoyance, but carried weight. Thus, to mention a single, outstanding example, it was as a result of his reading Schlegel's treatise that Schelling began to re-examine his own philosophic position, so that the book marks a milestone on his way to the final, religious phase of his thought.

VI *Friedrich Schlegel's Conversion*

Some six weeks before the treatise on India was published, Friedrich and Dorothea were solemnly accepted into the Catholic faith. The event surprised, and indeed scandalized, many a contemporary who had lost touch with Schlegel since the days of the *Athenäum*. It could have surprised no one who was familiar with the development of Schlegel's thoughts subsequent to his move to Paris.

As the history of the whole Romantic movement shows, the times were ripe for a religious revival. The German Enlightenment had brought with it, and indeed was in its essence, a process of increasing secularization of every conceivable field of human activity. There was the widespread, optimistic belief that any problem whatever could be solved by the powers of reasoning, that human intelligence could both produce and ensure the observance of a system of natural morality and, hence, that man had no need of supernatural tutelage. Yet when the Goddess of Reason was triumphantly enthroned in Paris, the Terror had already commenced; and, in Germany no less than in France, the age-old problems of suffering, evil, greed, and folly refused to yield to the sweet voice of reason. The basis for human actions and convictions provided by enlightened rationalism turned out to be less reliable than had been hoped, and people began, once again, to long for a less arduous path to certainty and for a more satisfying source of consolation and reassurance in times of trouble than secular systems of thought could provide.

"A human being needs something solid to which he can hold on," W. von Humboldt wrote to his wife on May 16, 1801:

something which provides him with a standard and an aim . . . , or else no value of any kind exists for him. In the whole realm of thought there is nothing that can serve this function. You connect one [idea] to another and that one to a third, and the mass of inter-connected things makes you believe that they can hold and support each other, but it is no use: the moments come when you feel that the whole chain is not attached to anything, and that the sole support for it all springs from your own heart . . .

In the 1790's, when Schlegel was full of hopes both for his own future and for that of the intellectual life of his country, he was still prepared to rely on his heart. "All theology is poetry," he wrote at that time. "Every God whose concept is not *made*, i.e., fully produced, by a man for himself, but is given to him, is—however sublime this concept may be—a mere idol."—"Religion is a matter of arbitrary choice." [31]

Moreover, he had hoped for a while that the new, Fichtean method of philosophy would achieve what the systems of the Enlightenment had failed to do. However, he had come to realize and reiterated time and again in his later writings that the Fichtean method of deduction from a rational principle led to nothing but "empty concepts and dead abstractions";[32] and when he drew on "poetry," i.e., on the imagination and on intuition, to supplement philosophy, he could hardly, in the long run, close his eyes to the fact that such a procedure threw man back entirely on his own resources. Behind the Fichtean system, there was the spectre of solipsism: "What is most frightening to man," Schlegel wrote in 1806, "is *absolute loneliness*. But Idealism is the very system in which the mind is completely isolated, bereft of everything that relates him to the ordinary world, so that it stands alone and completely deprived." [33]

To put matters differently, he came to realize that his doctrine of poetry as a source of knowledge depended on an external sanction—that "inspiration" presupposes a "spirit," that "enthusiasm" presupposes a "theos." In the end, as he gradually came to see, one could not avoid the necessity of deciding between the alternatives of a purely secular world of relative, uncertain, man-made values, and a world of faith and divine sanctions.[34] It is because of this realization and because of the fear of nihilism engendered by it that so many *aperçus* of the first half of his life remind one of Nietzsche.[35]

Nietzsche, of course, fought this fear by declaring that it was man's task to create his own values; and when Schlegel, in Berlin and Jena, insisted that man made his own Gods and that any God not so made was a mere idol, he was not too far removed from a Nietzschean position. But those were days when, buoyed up by his own achievements and full of high hopes for himself and mankind, he was persuaded that man could live by his own strength and was in need of no other guidance or consolation than that derived from his own ideals. In Paris, when he began to accept a God given to man, rather than created by man, as a symbol of his highest aspirations, those hopes had been thoroughly crushed.

The *Athenäum,* as the reader will remember, had ceased publication, and the Jena circle had dispersed. His play had failed on the stage and was savagely attacked by critics. In the course of his frantic efforts to add a second volume to his *Lucinde,* he had written a good many poems, but as he could not make up his mind on the general framework into which the poems would fit, work on his novel slowly ground to a halt. His hopes of establishing himself as the prophet of German Idealism "in partibus infidelium" [36] came to nothing, as did his hope of finding suitable employment. With so many failures and disappointments weighing on his mind, his dream of an imminent rejuvenation of mankind dissolved, and with it his faith in the self-reliance of man. The time to search for external support, for a different meaning to life, for supernatural sanctions and reassurances had come, and it so happened that all his major activities and experiences in Paris combined to guide this search in the same direction.

We have already seen how large a share of his efforts during his Paris years was devoted to the study of painting, and with what results. Suffice it now to point out that if his conviction of the symbolic nature of all art turned his attention to religious paintings, these paintings, in turn, convinced him of the superiority of Christian symbolism. It is probably a reflection of his own experience in the art galleries of Paris that many years later, when he attempted to convert the Comtesse de St. Aulaire to his own religious views, he used paintings as a means of persuasion. [37] Again, we have seen that his study of Sanskrit led him to the adoption of the degeneration theory of religion, that it thus helped to support his incipient belief in an original monotheistic revelation, and that he identified this revelation with that of the Pentateuch. It is in perfect agreement with these findings that in his later writings Christ is seen as the restorer of an original faith revealed once and for all rather than as a creator of a new faith.

Now for some time—possibly still toward the end of 1803—Schlegel vacillated between Catholicism and Protestantism; but the bias toward the former, or at any rate against the latter, was deeply rooted in the Romantic movement. German Enlightenment had its base in the Protestant North and had imbued Protestant thought with its rationalism. As Schlegel and his friends saw it, there was a kind of poetic justice in this: in their eyes, the

Enlightenment itself was a long-range result of the Reformation. According to Tieck, the Reformation had replaced the "fullness of a divine religion" by an "arid rational emptiness." [38] According to A. W. Schlegel, the Reformation had cut Christianity off "from its venerable origins [*Vorzeit*]" and had "destroyed the mythical world" of medieval Christendom.[39] The latter was celebrated by Novalis in *Die Christenheit oder Europa*, an essay so outspoken in its Catholic bias that A. W. Schlegel, afraid that it might cause a scandal and, with Goethe's support, vetoed its publication in the *Athenäum*.

Novalis' essay—a prose-poem masquerading as history—is more likely to irritate modern readers than to inspire them, but so many of its notions were gradually accepted by Schlegel that a few remarks about it may be helpful. It was in the Middle Ages, Novalis tells us, that Europe had been a genuinely "Christian country"—a single, "vast spiritual realm" united by "one great common interest" and one single spiritual Head. In those days, we are told, the princes of Europe "submitted their quarrels to the Father of Christendom and willingly laid their crowns . . . at his feet." Scientific discoveries were quite rightly opposed by the Church, lest they tempt believers to prefer "limited knowledge" to "infinite faith." The Reformation illustrates the harm inflicted by culture on the feeling for the infinite, or "at least the temporary harmfulness of culture at a certain stage." Accompanied by destructive wars— there is no hint, in Novalis' essay, at the struggles of Pope and Emperor that had rent the Middle Ages—the Reformation had "separated the inseparable Church" and thus created a "state of religious anarchy." Luther had "treated Christianity arbitrarily, misunderstood its spirit, and introduced a different letter and a different religion, i.e., the sacred general validity of the Bible," thus contaminating religion with the purely secular science of philology. "With the Reformation, Christianity was done for. It no longer existed." The inevitable result of the Reformation was the Enlightenment and our present religious, intellectual, and political anarchy, which must, however, lead to a new order: "True anarchy is the generative element of religion." Both Catholicism— at least in its present, corrupted form—and Protestantism will pass away, and a new, truly reformed Christianity will rise from the ashes, uniting Europe once again.

As the conclusion of his essay shows, Novalis did not advocate a return to the Middle Ages; but this was in 1799, when the Romantics were united in the expectation of a great European renaissance. And as he died in 1801, we have no way of knowing how he would have reacted to the collapse of these hopes. Both Tieck and A. W. Schlegel came very close to a conversion, but both turned away again from Catholicism and in their old age took up positions surprisingly close to that of the Enlightenment. Thus, it was left to Friedrich to carry his and his friends' common starting point to its logical conclusion.

How much of a difference it made that at the decisive moment, unlike his friends, he happened to live in a Catholic country, is hard to assess; but it was certainly important that his closest and most loyal friends at that time, the Boisserées and their traveling companion Bertram, were Catholics. Schlegel was bitterly hurt by the fact that Tieck and Schleiermacher had failed to help him with his periodical, and after he had left Paris, he was greatly moved by the kind reception he was given in Cologne, in spite of all his financial miseries. "If you think we are partial towards Catholicism," he wrote in February, 1806, to a Protestant acquaintance, "I must confess that this is partly due to personal friendship. It is only with these much-condemned people that I have found such general esteem and such heartfelt friendship. My former so-called friends, be they Calvinists, Lutherans or Moravians, theists, atheists or idealists, have—with the sole exception of my own brother, who is, however, a very bad Calvinist—behaved towards me like a veritable pack of gypsies." [40]

To such personal reasons must be added that at least Bertram, who was older and more knowledgeable than the Boisserées, was much more than a passive listener during the gatherings in Schlegel's home. What was decisive, however, was the kind of argument Novalis had put forward in his essay of 1799. "The new Christianity," Schlegel had jotted down at that time, "must, without doubt, be the Catholic one, but old Catholic, not Papism [altkatholisch, nicht Papsttum]." [41] The same conviction was expressed in an unpublished jotting of 1806, in which Schlegel distinguished "four ages of the Catholic religion: 1. strict virtue, 2. naïve faith in externals, 400–1000, 3. culpable self-assurance [Sicherheit] and indiscretion, 1000–1500, 4. hypocrisy—since the Reformation. One can almost say that religion does no longer exist." [42] Thus, the right way appeared to be the way back—in accordance with that pessimistic view of history with which we are already familiar. "That which is original [*ursprünglich*] in all things is certainly the best," Schlegel announced in his Lessing anthology, adding that this maxim was particularly true of religion, which was "by no means an innovation of modern times, but is itself the first and most ancient [source] of all human culture and freedom." [43] And the way back could only be found through Catholicism: the original revelation had been restored by Christ, and Christ's teachings were preserved—so Schlegel came to believe around 1804—in the living tradition of the Catholic Church, which was superior to Protestantism because its tradition was unbroken. Dorothea, always her husband's faithful echo, sums it all up in a nutshell: "If only because it is so ancient, I prefer Catholicism. Nothing new is of any use." [44]

In 1806, Friedrich began to prepare himself for the formal act of conversion by the study of the Church Fathers and of scholastic philosophy. In the following year, he tried to make arrangements for the *professio fidei*, but as Dorothea was a divorcee, special permission had to be obtained, and the ceremony was delayed till April, 1808. Two weeks later, he left Cologne.

CHAPTER 6

Romantic Politics

I *Romantic Conservatism*

IN Berlin, Jena, and Paris, as we have seen, Schlegel had considered the *Roman* the most suitable vehicle of romantic poetry, though—prompted by his admiration for Calderón, whom the Schlegels rescued from oblivion—he had also tried his hand at writing a play. Subsequently, particularly in Cologne, where he planned to dramatize the life of Emperor Charles V, he became increasingly interested in the possibilities of romantic drama. Later still, he came to feel that the epic was best suited to fulfill the most significant functions of poetry, and toward the end of his life he exhausted the possibilities by giving pride of place to lyrical poetry.

His studies for the projected plays on Charles V made it desirable for Schlegel to consult the Imperial Archives in Vienna, but there were also other, no less urgent reasons for him to visit the Austrian capital. In the 1790's, he had been an ardent partisan of the French Revolution, and when Napoleon grasped the reigns of power, he had transferred at least some of his enthusiasm to the great Corsican. But as his view of history changed and his religious convictions strengthened, his politics underwent a radical transformation. Thus, when tensions arose between the Pope and Napoleon in the winter of 1803/1804, two years after the Concordat, Schlegel gradually turned against the French emperor. Having begun to look to the Middle Ages for guidance in politics as well as in religion, he had lost faith in the ideals the French Revolution had stood for and now saw in its heir not only an enemy of his own country, but an enemy of all law and order. "Lest all government and all human decency be destroyed," he wrote in his Lessing anthology, "the one thing needful is that old law and old custom, honor and liberty and the dignity of sovereigns be retained . . . and restored." [1] The reformer was turning into a champion of the old order, the cosmopolitan into a German patriot.

But what was "Germany"? No German national state was in existence; large parts of German territory, including Cologne, had been annexed by the French, and numerous German rulers supported Napoleon for their own selfish purposes. Moreover, Schlegel was a Hanoverian by birth, and Hanover was ruled in personal union by the sovereign of Great Britain. Under such circumstances, and given the Romantic predilection for the Middle Ages, Schlegel's patriotism was practically bound to focus on the Holy Roman Empire, or, after 1806, on such traditions and reminiscences as were left of it. Now this empire had been ruled for centuries by the Hapsburgs; and as the Napoleonic wars spread across Europe, it seemed to Schlegel, with some justification, that it was the Hapsburgs more than any other German sovereign who persistently opposed Napoleon and the revolutionary spirit he represented—a spirit which Schlegel now increasingly tended to identify with materialism and atheism.

Austria, he wrote in January, 1806, was "the only state still concerned with the preservation of what is good and old," [2] while Prussia, which had not joined the Third Coalition, and Russia, on which he blamed the French victory at Austerlitz, called forth his ire and contempt. Moreover, it was Austria that seemed to him the depository of the best traditions of the Holy Roman Empire. "Austria," he wrote in February of the same year, "is the only country where there is still liberty, the only liberty which is worth anything, i.e., that based on the estates of the realm . . . ; in England, liberty is nothing but comedy and pretense, and liberty in America is merely that of calves who end up by going to the stable." [3] A multi-nation state united—as it seemed to Schlegel— at once by loyalty to the Emperor and in the spirit of Christ, Austria seemed to him the embodiment of that synthesis of unity and variety that he looked for in politics as everywhere else, and the only possible model for a new order in Europe, if such an order was ever to arise out of its present chaos. If there was any state he now wanted to serve, it was Austria.

Yet another reason that made a visit to Vienna seem desirable was the fact that A. W. Schlegel visited the city in spring, 1808, gave a series of lectures—the famous lectures *Über dramatische*

Kunst und Literatur—and was not only very warmly acclaimed, but made a handsome profit.

Even so, Schlegel at first only thought of a temporary stay in Austria. Having left Cologne toward the end of April, he used the opportunity to visit old friends on the way, among them his brother and Mme de Staël, whom he met in Dresden; he arrived in Vienna on June 22. Although his reputation as the frivolous author of *Lucinde* still dogged his footsteps wherever he went, his reception was kindly, and he soon found influential friends. An ardent Catholic, Baron Josef Penkler, introduced him to the Redemptorist Father Hofbauer—now the Patron Saint of Vienna —to whose religious circle he belonged for the rest of his life, deriving from it not only spiritual guidance, but practical help. Among its members were the influential civil servant J. A. von Pilat, the beautiful Countess Julie Zichy, who had excellent connections in high places, and—at a later stage—the dramatist Zacharias Werner, a fellow convert (1810), who in 1814 became a priest. It was through Hofbauer's circle that Schlegel was put in touch with the papal nuncio Severoli and, after 1815, with Crown Prince Ludwig of Bavaria. He made friends with the Austrian historian Hormayr and was recommended to Metternich, who in turn introduced him to Count Stadion.

Reassured, by such personal contacts, that he would be able to attract numerous listeners from among the nobility, Schlegel made arrangements for a public course of lectures on European history, when the resumption of hostilities between France and Austria suddenly changed his plans: On March 28, 1809, he was appointed to a position in the Austrian civil service with the rank of a *Hofsekretär* and was attached to Count Stadion's headquarters with the Austrian army in Bavaria. In June, when Napoleon had occupied Vienna and thus gained control of the Austrian government's main organ of publicity, the *Wiener Zeitung*, it became Schlegel's task to create a substitute, the *Österreichische Zeitung*, which he edited at the Army Headquarters from June 24 to December 16. He was an eyewitness of the battles of Aspern and Wagram, retreated with the Army Headquarters to Hungary, where Dorothea joined him for a while, and did not return to Vienna till December 18.

The reaccommodation between France and Austria after the Peace of Vienna made overt political activity—now his major interest—difficult for the avowed enemy of Napoleon, but he played a significant role in founding the sequel to the *Österreichische Zeitung*, the *Österreichische Beobachter*, which became the most important Austrian newspaper of the era of Metternich. For ten months—until December 31, 1810—he was the official editor of this paper, though in fact he was only in control of its less important, cultural section.

In the meantime, he had obtained permission to give his series of lectures on European history, which he held, at first twice, then three times weekly, from February 19 to May 9.[4] As he wrote to Boisserée, he had 162 subscribers, among them "about twenty duchesses and princesses,"[5] a fact which reflects both the excellent work done by Schlegel's friends among the nobility—who turned the lectures into a social occasion—and the steepness of the subscription fee (30 fl.). An anonymous reviewer subsequently remarked that one could tell from the text of these lectures to what audience they were addressed,[6] but this is hardly fair criticism. Schlegel did not profess pro-Austrian views because he lectured in Vienna, but was in Vienna because he held pro-Austrian views. In fact, his lectures have to be read under a double perspective: as straight history, as which they are of minor importance; and as a presentation of Schlegel's political philosophy, which is of considerable interest.

Schlegel began with some brief remarks on the history of Rome, making the surprisingly modern, Orwellian suggestion that the Roman patricians constantly waged war abroad so as to perpetuate their despotic rule at home more easily. In dealing with the Great Migrations, he spoke at length about the political constitution of the Germanic tribes and struck the keynote of his whole course of lectures:

Nobility and freedom were the foundation of the earliest Germanic constitution. . . . In no nation do we find the nobility—the first of all the estates, foundation of every constitution based on the estates, first and most essential natural element of the true state—characterized by such grand and striking qualities, and placed in such perfect relations [with the rest of the nation], as among the Germans. This is one reason why their earliest history is so instructive. . . . In this respect, it may be said that German history, from the earliest to the most recent times, is a natural and most instructive theory of the true state, i.e., of the constitution based on the estates.[7]

The importance of Charlemagne is seen in his activities as a legislator rather than as a conqueror—above all in his having raised the clergy to a position of sufficient power to balance that of the nobility. This balance of secular and spiritual power is an essential element of Schlegel's conservative and restorative politics and determines his conception of the political and cultural role of the Pope:

The Papal power, like the Imperial, was a popular one; the Pope was the spokesman and umpire of the European republic, which was already felt to be a want, although it was not yet set up as a distinct ideal. This contributed much to the peculiar character of the European civilization; for, by this very influence of the Popes, the European nations were placed in close communion, yet without losing their independence. Here, in fact, was first manifested that ideal which is the foundation of the European system of states and nations—the ideal of a rightful union, of a free confederacy—which should embrace all nations and states of the civilized world, without sacrificing the unity, the free and peculiar national development of any individual nation.[8]

Schlegel frankly admitted that the ideal of a free confederacy of European states under the guidance of Pope and Emperor had not been brought to full perfection either in the Middle Ages or at later times, but he had no need of an idealized picture of the past to drive home his lesson for the present: if the Holy Roman Empire and the Hapsburg multi-nation monarchy, with all their faults and shortcomings, were modeled on the right idea—the free interplay of unity and variety—Napoleonic despotism was its very antithesis. And while any direct attack on the French emperor would have been utter folly at the very time when the marriage of Napoleon and Marie Louise (April, 1810) was cementing an enforced alliance between France and Austria, Schlegel knew that his audience could be relied upon to grasp his allusions. The "power of the German king and emperor," he insisted time and again, "was a popular power that reposed entirely upon the force of public opinion, upon faith in the loftiness of the imperial office, upon veneration for its sanctity."[9] The "Austrian sovereigns" from Albert II to Charles V were guided by the "concept of a Christian republic, of a free and peaceable confederation of all European states and nations"—a very different ideal indeed from those of "other European kings," whose sole aim was the consolidation of their own, absolute power.[10] And if the Austrian emperors thus could be relied upon not to abuse their position, the very reverse was true of those "other monarchs" whose foreign policy was not based on the model of a federative, multi-nation structure at home:

> The history of the world teaches . . . that some central point is necessary in an aggregate of states and nations that, like those in Europe, have stood for centuries in an intercourse so close, so complex, geographically and morally so inevitable and indispensable—some central point whence a supreme directing influence may radiate over the whole body. Hence the question is not whether such influence shall exist, for it has always existed, and always will do so; but of what nature it shall be, by whom and how it shall be exercised, is the problem on which the freedom of the whole body politic depends. . . . By its own nature the imperial supremacy (if it is permissible, in the language of the Middle Ages, thus to call that supreme influence over the free association of Christian states)—an influence defined and moulded as it was by religious and moral principles and objectives— . . . was in its own essence by no means an encroachment on the general freedom of Europe, or a form of injustice. The false imperial supremacy, however, that supremacy which does not proceed from, and is not based on, moral and religious ideas, but upon the dead mechanism of mere selfish despotism, is indeed the greatest misfortune which can befall mankind.[11]

No lecturer, speaking in Vienna in 1810, with a police agent in the audience, could afford plainer language.

II *The Lectures on Ancient and Modern Literature*

Encouraged by the success of his lectures on history, Schlegel applied in the fall of 1810 for permission to hold a similar lecture course on literature, with the title *Geschichte der alten und neuen Literatur*. As his application was opposed both by the University of Vienna, whose philosophical faculty was still dominated by partisans of the Enlightenment, and by police officials, who were worried about Schlegel's anti-French views, permission was not granted till the following June. It was only now that his friends could embark on the task of attracting subscribers, so that Schlegel could devote the whole of 1811 to preparing himself. He lectured twice a week, from February 27 to April 30, 1812, in the ballroom of a fashionable hotel in the inner city. As in 1810, his public consisted to a large extent of the high Austrian nobility; and as before, the political circumstances of the day greatly influenced the tone and content of his lectures, which commenced four months before Napoleon's declaration of war on Russia and a year before Prussia's declaration of war against Napoleon. It seems due to these circumstances that Schlegel laid so much stress on the patriotic function of poetry—an emphasis that was balanced by an equally pronounced emphasis on its religious function in the second, revised version of these lectures, published in 1822.

"The most important factor for the whole further development and indeed for the whole intellectual life of a nation," Schlegel asserts in his first lecture, ". . . is its possession of a rich store of grand national traditions, . . . the preservation and glorification of which is the foremost task of poetry." [12] Starting from this assumption, he arrives at a classification of poetry which—contrary to his earlier views—gives pride of place to the epic, and in particular to such medieval heroic poems as the *Nibelungenlied:*

> The first and original function of poetry, with respect . . . to the service it is to render to a nation, is to preserve and embellish its national reminiscences and myths, and to celebrate and perpetuate in the memory its glorious past; this is the case in heroic poems, where free scope is given to the miraculous, and where the poet can draw on mythology. The second function of poetry is to set before men's eyes a distinct and lively portraiture of actual life. This can be done most vividly in the drama. . . . [But] it is not only the outward manifestations of life that poetry is intended to mirror; it can also serve to arouse the higher life of inward feeling. The essence of poetry devoted to this latter function is enthusiasm—that more exalted and more beautiful state of feeling that can manifest itself in many shapes and forms, which, however, as soon as this aspect predominates, will all belong to the lyric genre.[13]

It follows from this primary function of poetry that all imitation of foreign literatures is wrong in principle; but Schlegel was convinced that the proper, consistent attachment to a national tradition would of itself ultimately transcend excessively narrow national boundaries:

> The imitation of another nation never attains its object; for everything produced by the latter in the epoch of its highest perfection and of its greatest achievement in the arts must always remain foreign to the

imitator. But every nation need only go back to its own original and most ancient poetry and myth. The nearer this source is arrived at and the more deeply it is tapped, the more conspicuous will those features be that are common to all nations. The national literatures, like the nations themselves, approximate one another in their origins.[14]

What Schlegel here preaches was already practiced by the second, younger generation of Romantic poets, who sought inspiration in German folk songs and medieval legends, and by Romantic scholars, who—after the pioneering ventures of such men as J. J. Bodmer and C. H. Myller—were laboring to make the German medieval epic a favorite subject of scholarship and a living, influential part of Germany's cultural heritage. Schlegel's literary nationalism—particularly his insistence that "every free and important nation has, as it were, the right to a literature of its own," [15] in its own language, and based on its own tradition—can hardly be claimed to constitute an advance on Herder's much earlier utterances in this vein, but helped some smaller European nations to gain confidence in their own literary efforts.

As regards his own earlier theories, it is evident that the *Roman* no longer had the central position in his system which it had previously occupied; but Schlegel still adhered to some of the most important convictions embodied in this theory of the *Roman* of 1800. While he now assigned the preservation of myth and national traditions primarily to the epic, the portraiture of actual life to the drama, and the expression of exalted feeling to the lyric, he still felt that all three functions had to be combined in the perfect work and thus still professed his old ideal of "universal poetry." In fact, all that had happened to his earlier theory of romantic poetry can be summed up under four headings: he had lost interest in contemporary prose fiction, except when it dealt with historical or legendary subjects; his former cosmopolitanism had been replaced by the patriotic outlook engendered by the Napoleonic wars; his theory was reformulated so as to bring it into line with his Christian convictions; and he was now less interested in the contrast between classical and romantic poetry and far more concerned with that between "genuine" poetry—i.e., poetry reflecting attitudes to the world compatible with his own, whether it be classical or romantic—and "false," *merely* modern poetry, which reflected the empiricist outlook of the Enlightenment.

Thus, it will be remembered, he had explained in the "Gespräch über die Poesie" that romantic poetry was "fantastic," "sentimental," and based on historical facts. In his lectures of 1812, this view is presented as follows:

There is but one general standard of criticism for the great mass of romantic poetry written at this time [after the Crusades]. . . . Their value is so much the higher in proportion as they rest on a *historical foundation,* and have a national import and character; in proportion also as they exhibit, in an unconstrained and natural manner, the wonderful in poetry, this being the proper sphere for the free play of *imagination;* and in proportion as they, in their totality, express the *spirit of love.* I mean by this not merely a gentle, considerate and as it were, loving treatment of everything that is represented, but rather the spirit which essentially distinguishes all genuinely Christian poetry.[16]

In view of his increasing emphasis on the Christian element in poetry, Schlegel might have been expected to exhibit a special predilection for works with an overtly theological theme, such as the epics of Dante, Milton, and Klopstock; but in spite of his admiration for the great Italian and his just and generous evaluation of Klopstock as one of the great founders of German eighteenth-century literature, he felt that a direct representation of the Christian religion in literature was inadvisable. "Christianity itself," he maintained, was not philosophy, but "that on which all philosophy is based"; it was not poetry, but "that which transcends all poetry, and whose spirit must, consequently, rule here as everywhere, but rule invisibly." [17] It is to be represented indirectly, through the spirit of love, as is the case, for instance, in the plays of Calderón.

It is in connection with Calderón that Schlegel expounds his theory of drama—a theory based on a distinction between three kinds of play. In the least valuable of these, only the "glittering surface of life" is presented. In the second kind, we are given a delineation of characteristics "not only of individuals, but of the whole, where the world and life are shown in all their variety, in their contradictions and their perplexing intricacies, where man and his existence, this most intricate enigma, are shown as such, as an enigma." If this were the supreme purpose of drama, Schlegel continues, Shakespeare would be by far the greatest playwright of all times. There is, however, a third and superior kind of drama, which shows how "the eternal emerges from mortal catastrophe," and which thus "not only presents, but solves the enigma of life"; the past master of this, the highest form of drama, is Calderón.

In an approximate parallel with these three types of drama, Schlegel also distinguishes between three types of tragic conclusion. The lowest is that in which the hero is utterly crushed, like Shakespeare's Macbeth and Schiller's Wallenstein. This is the type predominant among the ancients. The second type ends with a kind of expiation or "Versöhnung," and is occasionally represented among the ancients. Thus Aeschylus, having disclosed the abyss of suffering and crime in the *Agamemnon* and in the *Choephoroi,* added the *Eumenides,* in which Orestes finds peace once more; and Sophocles wrote not only *Oedipus Rex,* but *Oedipus at Colonus,* where the unhappy king's death is shown in such a beautiful light as to leave us with feelings more pensive than painful. The third and highest type of dramatic conclusion is that "in which extreme suffering issues in a state of spiritual transfiguration." This type, Schlegel tells us, is especially suited to Christian poets, and Calderón is its most eminent exponent. He is "under every condition and circumstance, and among all dramatic poets, the most Christian, and for that reason the most romantic." [18]

Thus, it will be noticed, the term "romantic" had assumed quite specifically Christian connotations in Schlegel's theory; but as he felt, in 1812 no less than in 1800, that all true poetry was to some extent romantic, and as he still loved and admired the Greeks, his terminology, and indeed his entire system, was less consistent than he seems to have realized. This inconsistency is clearly brought out in the twelfth of his *Lectures,* where he made his most determined attempt at defining his central term. The romantic, we are here told,

is based solely on the sentiment of love that predominates along with Christianity and through Christianity also in poetry—that love in which even suffering only appears as a means of transfiguration, the tragic earnestness of ancient mythology and pagan antiquity being dissolved into serene playfulness of the imagination, and those external forms of representation and language being selected that correspond to the inward sentiment of love and the playfulness of the imagination.

So far, Schlegel—paraphrasing, once again, his old definition of romantic poetry as that which presents a sentimental subject in a fantastic form—is perfectly consistent; but then he continues:

> In this sense, in which the romantic designates only the specifically Christian beauty and poetry, all poetry ought to be romantic. In fact, the romantic as such does not conflict with the . . . genuinely ancient. The legend of Troy and the Homeric lays are thoroughly romantic, as is everything that is truly poetic in Indian, Persian and other ancient oriental or European poems.

Thus, Schlegel was driven by the logic of his own argument to ascribing Christian sentiments of love and "specifically Christian beauty" to the Homeric epics and to Indian and Persian poetry. He himself must have felt that he was treading on rather thin ice; for he continued, not without a touch of embarrassment:

> Wherever the highest life is comprehended and portrayed feelingly and with enthusiastic presentiment of its profounder significance, there are at least some intimations of that divine love whose center and whose full harmony is indeed only found in Christianity. Intimations of this sentiment are widespread even with the ancient tragedians, in spite of their predominantly dark and gloomy philosophy. Inward love will spring forth in noble minds even in the midst of error and false images of horror. It is not only the artistry of Aeschylus and Sophocles that is great and admirable, but also their way of thinking and feeling. . . . Thus the romantic does not contrast with genuine antiquity, but only with the pseudo-classicism that is held up to us as a model, with everything that merely apes the form of the ancients without inward love; it is also opposed to the modern, which falsely seeks to influence life by slavishly adhering to the present and confining itself to the actual, with the result that, however refined its aim or its subject may be, it inevitaby succumbs to the tyranny of fleeting time and fashion.[19]

In the late 1790's, Schlegel had been in the vanguard of his time, and although even then his greatest love had belonged to the literature of the past, he had not only initiated a literary movement of European significance, but had correctly foreseen the trend of contemporary literature. In particular, he had been among the very few critics who realized the increasing impor- tance of the novel as a literary form, and his theory of the *Roman* had anticipated a good many features that were embodied in the experimental novels of the twentieth century.[20] Now, he was fighting a rearguard action. Despite the Romantic movement, which was still gathering strength, nineteenth-century literature as a whole was irrevocably moving in a direction which Schlegel abhorred: toward greater realism or—as he himself would have put it—toward greater "empiricism." Even so, it can hardly be denied that Schlegel's *Geschichte der alten und neuen Literatur* ranks as a major achievement. It is based on a knowledge of world literature that has rarely been equalled; it presents a canon that is remarkably fair even to such un-Romantic movements as French classicism; and it paints a picture of the organic growth and development of literature that was far ahead of its time. In the words of Wellek and Warren, these lectures, along with A. W. Schlegel's surveys, may still be the only histories of world literature to have "gone beyond ideological generalities or superficial compilations." [21]

The lectures were printed in 1815 and subsequently translated into French, English, Spanish, Italian, Polish, and Swedish. The first, abridged, English translation of 1818 was twice reprinted and was re-edited in Philadelphia "with a series of questions for examinations in schools." A second, complete translation into English, based on the enlarged German version of 1822, appeared in 1859 and was reprinted in 1865, 1871, 1876, and 1896. The Italian edition (1828) was reissued five times within thirty years. Thus, Schlegel's *Geschichte der alten und neuen Literatur* served its century well. Today, it is hopelessly out of date; but the scholarship that has rendered it antiquated is signally indebted to it for methodological refinement and stimulation.

III *The Congress of Vienna and the Diet of Frankfort*

In 1811, when Schlegel was preparing his lectures on world literature, he had also done the spade work for a new journalistic venture: he had founded a literary monthly, the *Deutsches Museum*, which appeared in twenty-four issues from the beginning of 1812 to the end of 1813. As Schlegel himself explained, this periodical was devoted to the "discussion and promotion of history and philosophy, art and literature, in a patriotic and thoroughly German spirit." [22] This time, he was highly successful in attracting prominent writers: the list of contributors includes A. W. Schlegel, Adam Müller, Matthias Claudius, Jean Paul, the brothers

Grimm, J. G. G. Büsching, Zacharias Werner, Fouqué, Matthäus von Collin, Wilhelm von Humboldt, Theodor Körner, Josef Görres, Christian Graf zu Stolberg, and Mme de Staël.[23] Among Schlegel's own contributions, a review of a recent publication by Jacobi, *Von den göttlichen Dingen und ihrer Offenbarung* (1811), is perhaps the most significant: it contains the first uncompromising public avowal of his conviction that philosophy must not start with a *tabula rasa,* like the deductive systems of Fichte and Schelling, but with the fact of a positive revelation.

In the meantime, Napoleon had invaded Russia and suffered catastrophic defeat; the Prussians had joined the Czar in his campaign in Germany, and Schlegel was longing for overt political activity. His opportunity came when Austria at long last declared war on France. By October, 1813, he could report to his brother that he was politically active again and indeed "a politically important person," "involved in very important commissions and labors dealing with the political situation in Germany." [24] Apparently Metternich had asked him to make proposals for the future constitution of Germany.[25] His drafts for these proposals are still unpublished, but his letters suggest that he wanted an "entirely new" constitution that yet preserved strong links with the past. The "proper basis of a German constitution and the German way of life," he thought, were to be found in the provincial diets; the power of the territorial rulers (but not of the Emperor) had to be controlled, for the independence of "that *canaille*," their treachery and stupidity had cost Germany its freedom.[26]

During the Congress of Vienna, Schlegel was instructed by Metternich to publish articles presenting an Austrian point of view in North German newspapers,[27] and he used his widespread personal connections to further the interests of the Church, which he served with far greater loyalty than was convenient to Metternich.[28] Among his most frequent contacts were Freiherr vom Stein, Wilhelm von Humboldt, and Friedrich Gentz; and he was called upon for advice and information by the papal nuncio Severoli, as well as by Cardinal Gonsalvi. According to an eyewitness, Varnhagen von Ense, "many diplomats liked to let themselves be instructed and advised [by Schlegel], but rarely found the advice useful"—a sally which, in view of Schlegel's ultramontanism, is not wholly unjustified. But the Church rewarded Schlegel for his efforts with one of its highest distinctions, the Order of Christ, and the Austrian government must also have found him useful. In October, 1815, Metternich let himself be persuaded to reactivate Schlegel's position in the civil service and nominated him First Secretary of the Austrian Legation to the Diet of Frankfort.

Ever since he had come to Vienna, Schlegel had been impressed by the practical advantages of belonging to the nobility. Now that he was about to embark on a career as a diplomat, he decided to make use of the fact that his great-grandfather, Christoph Schlegel, had been ennobled by Ferdinand III and had adopted the predicate *von Gottleben*. The title having since fallen into disuse, Friedrich petitioned Francis II for permission to revive it, and though he never received an answer, henceforth styled himself Friedrich von Schlegel.[29]

In Frankfort, Schlegel became involved in the local politics of the city, wrote reports on the Diet for North German newspapers, and agitated for the civil rights of the German Jews. His most persistent efforts were again devoted to the interests of the Church, but his extremism turned out to be self-defeating. In the view of his superior, Count Buol-Schauenstein—whom Schlegel, to be sure, considered to be a "complete imbecile and, moreover, a most obstinate person of the most objectionable character"[30]—he neglected his official duties and propagated views of such eccentricity as to cause embarrassment to his employers; and Gentz, who had known him for close to twenty years and in many ways admired and respected him, now wrote in unmitigated fury that Schlegel had "never had any talent for practical matters," and that in more recent years his "religious, or rather, ecclesiastical frenzy had turned him into an utter fool."[31] Gradually, it became obvious to Metternich that Schlegel's presence in Frankfort did the Austrian cause more harm than good. In April, 1818, he was officially recalled, but he had lived beyond his means during the last three years and was so heavily in debt that he could only leave town after lengthy and embarrassing financial negotiations. It was not until November that he arrived back in Vienna, convinced, at long last, that politics was not his game.

CHAPTER 7

The Final Phase

I *Personal Failings*

IN many ways, as we have seen, the first eighteen years of the new century had been years of impressive achievement for Friedrich Schlegel. He had significantly influenced the theory and practice of painting, pioneered a juster appraisal of Gothic architecture, and become the founder of Sanskrit studies in Germany. He had lectured at length on philosophy, established himself as a historian, and published a history of literature that was gaining him international recognition. He had enjoyed an opportunity to try his hand as a diplomat and had been awarded a rare distinction by the Pope. Yet in other ways, these years had brought him a dismal series of failures and disappointments. Both *Europa* and the *Deutsches Museum* had proved financial liabilities and had to cease publication. The countless plans for plays, novels, and epics he had entertained since 1802 had all failed to materialize, and the poems he had published had been condemned by the majority of his critics. His efforts as a scholar had not procured him a professorship, and his diplomatic activities had ended with his being retired at the age of forty-five. His conversion had made him many enemies in North Germany, and his enchantment with Austria had turned into bitter disappointment. "You are speaking of Germany," he wrote to Dorothea, who was with her sons in Italy, in June, 1819. "Alas, if only I were there, if I could live there . . . But how do you arrive at the strange notion that Vienna is in Germany, or has anything to do with Germany? Whole continents lie between them, and there can hardly be a greater contrast. . . ." [1] Also, Schlegel was once again in financial difficulties. The earnings from his lectures of 1812 had been paid in inflationary currency,[2] and in Frankfort, his salary had proved inadequate.[3] He was now receiving a pension, but was hounded by old and new debts contracted at high rates of interest, and he was an inveterate spendthrift.

Worst of all, he was not the kind of man who stands up well under pressure. Ever since the dispersion of the Jena circle, he had suffered from fits of depression; from about 1803 onward, he hardly ever commented on his own state of mind in his letters except to complain. Thus he tells his brother in July, 1804, that he is "sad and depressed." [4] In the following winter, he reports to Mme de Staël that he is "triste, vexé, las . . . Une douleur calme et toujours égale règne dans la nuit de mon cœur." [5] Next spring, he writes that "life, the world, and above all I myself have become matters of such indifference to me that it costs me an effort to take an interest in anything at all, and that I do so only out of a sense of duty." [6] A year later, he has been "indescribably sad and out-of-sorts for months." [7] His move to Vienna seemed to have a tonic effect on him, but this did not last. In January, 1810, he suffers from an "almost insuperable sadness" that inhibits all springs of action and renders him indifferent to the world.[8] In the fall of the same year, he complains of his "despondency, sadness, dismay and anxiety," suggests that his "melancholy" might be due to ill health, and adds, significantly enough: "I have now come to realize that the spleen can be a real physical sickness; all doctors agree with me, and treat me for hypochondria." [9] Next March, he is still weighed down by the same inexplicable sadness,[10] and in the following June, Dorothea writes in despair that she is helplessly watching her husband perish in a vicious circle of "failure, sickness and grief." [11]

In 1812, his state of mind temporarily improved, but despondency soon set in again, and from then on he was its constant victim. There would be no point in adducing a long string of quotations.[12] A single passage tells the whole story: Schlegel's health, Dorothea wrote to a friend in July, 1821, was so poor as to interfere with his work. "The slow progress he is making," she continues, "depresses him, his depression aggravates his ill health; and so there results a vicious circle from which we cannot escape, which causes us much grief and great worries, and which prevents the execution of any ambitious plans." [13]

Schlegel's ill health, in turn, was aggravated by his undisciplined way of life. From the turn of the century onward, he had begun to develop a fondness for good wines, and he gradually fell into the habit of consoling himself in his troubles by consuming vast quantities of food. As early as 1804, Benjamin Constant described him as "un petit homme rond, gras outre mesure."[14] By 1812, Schlegel, who used to rise at dawn and work till late into the night, began to stay in bed till ten or half-past ten, and had become so fat that former friends failed to recognize him. The notes which the Viennese police spies compiled on him during the Congress of Vienna make depressing reading. "Hofsecretär Schlegel," they report, "for over a week has made a habit of refreshing himself with wine several times a day, and uses several places for this purpose. These are the café in the Herrengasse, the café Benko in the Stefansplatz, the wine-shop 'Zur Rose' . . . , Lenky's in the Liliengasse, and Reich's in the Hohe Markt . . . On the 15th [July, 1814] he visited all five of these places one after another and partook of refreshments . . ."[15] In Frankfort, Gentz was told that Schlegel could not get through the day on less than five meals and three bottles of wine, and found him completely apathetic and looking fifteen years older than August Wilhelm.[16] Another acquaintance, Franz von Baader, quipped: "C'est un esprit tombé de l'empyrée dans une cuisine."[17]

During the last eight years of his life, Schlegel lived more moderately, but now had another preoccupation that proved no less harmful to his public image. Among the characteristics of the German Romantic movement in its later stages was a pronounced interest in occult phenomena. With Schlegel, this interest centered in mesmerism or animal magnetism, to which he was introduced in the fall of 1818. He considered "magnetism" to be a special gift bestowed by God on individual believers to be used for the purpose of faith-healing, and soon convinced himself that he himself had special curative powers and enjoyed, to a limited extent and in privileged moments, the gift of clairvoyance.[18]

Most of our information about Schlegel's interest in animal magnetism comes from the long letters he wrote between January, 1821 and the time of his death to Christine von Stransky, who shared his preoccupation. Schlegel and Christine had met briefly in 1808 and had persuaded themselves that there was a mystical bond between them, but almost lost touch with each other in the following twelve years. During the years of their intensive correspondence, they arranged hours for simultaneous prayer intended to put them in telepathic contact and used their supposed "magnetic" insight to advise each other both in spiritual and practical matters. As Christine suffered from a variety of ailments, mostly of neurasthenic origin, Schlegel attempted to treat her, but on the only two occasions on which they saw each other again, in 1825 and 1827, he seems to have done more harm than good: both times, Christine developed painful stigmata after Schlegel's departure. At other times, from 1821 onward, he treated her, harmlessly enough, at a distance, sending her "magnetized" cotton, locks of hair, and even a piece of a tooth. If all this strikes the modern reader as somewhat ludicrous, it must be remembered that such practices were widespread in the first half of the nineteenth century. Schlegel's physician, Giovanni Malfatti—to cite one example of many—used similar methods of treatment and, for many years, was the most fashionable doctor among the Viennese nobility.[19] C. T. H. Windischmann, who seems to have introduced Schlegel to the practice of faith-healing, was a respected professor of medicine and philosophy at the University of Bonn, and the literature on "magnetic" cures written in Germany at that time by professional physicians is vast.

II Concordia

Oddly enough, Schlegel's dabblings in occultism helped rather than hindered his return to a more productive way of life. Convinced that his study of "magnetic" phenomena endowed him with special insights, particularly in matters of faith, he now overcame his reticence to acquaint a wider, possibly hostile public with the results of his lifelong study of philosophy.

In the winter of 1815/16, Schlegel had begun to make plans for a new periodical, his fourth and last; but when, almost two years later, he announced his intentions in a prospectus, the project was vetoed by Metternich. Schlegel's retirement from government service enabled him, however, to revive his plans and to produce six issues of what was intended to be a monthly, the first five appearing more or less on time from August through December, 1820, while the sixth was not published till April, 1823.[20] In Frankfort, Schlegel had decided to call his periodical *Concordia*, this title being intended to express the hope that his new venture might help to promote concord between the various branches of Christendom and bridge the schism caused by the Reformation. Accordingly, he had counted on the cooperation of such Protestant authors as A. W. Schlegel and Schleiermacher. When his plans finally materialized, he retained the old title, but his intentions had changed. As he explained in the very first sentence of his new periodical, its purpose was to provide an analysis of the "total moral condition of our age" by a "considerable number of scholars and scientifically trained men in Austria and the rest of *Catholic* Germany"—though he was cautious enough to add that he would "everywhere show the greatest respect for the thoroughly learned, truly Christian and pious Protestants." [21]

Schlegel himself contributed two major essays, "Signatur des Zeitalters" and "Von der Seele," an interesting discussion of the religious poetry of Lamartine—who is celebrated as the greatest living French poet—and some minor pieces. There is little in "Von der Seele" that Schlegel did not say again in greater detail in his lectures of 1827 and 1828; but the other essay, "Signatur des Zeitalters," [22] which, with its 150 pages, dominates the whole periodical, is so vivid an expression of the political position Schlegel had now reached that a brief discussion of it will be useful.

Schlegel begins by deploring that, while external peace had been achieved with the defeat of Napoleon, inner discord, party strife, and personal unhappiness prevailed throughout Europe. The origins of this spiritual malaise, according to Schlegel, were not to be found exclusively in the "false theories and pernicious systems of the eighteenth century";[23] indeed, the French Revolution had only been "a particular symptom, a partial outbreak, a first crisis" of a far more fundamental disease—the "religious, moral and political unbelief of the age." [24] Faith and love were only aroused and preserved by faith and love, and hence the disease could only be healed by positive teachings, not by polemics. Such polemics were, however, the dominant mode of political expression; in fact, it was the curse of the age that nothing was considered dispassionately, everything becoming immediately a matter of party strife and faction.

A "limitless striving" for the chimeras of "absolute unity and absolute liberty" poisoned the atmosphere, the former leading to the deductive philosophical systems that denied a personal god, the latter leading to the general and no less pernicious clamor for parliamentary systems along British or American lines—a veritable "English sickness." [25] But pernicious extremism was to be found among the protagonists of the right as well as the wrong ideas, among the "ultras" as well as the liberals. They both shared the common error of promoting the concept of a "purely mathematical, merely mechanical and machine-like" state that—whether it be the absolutism of a Louis XIV or that of an elected government—rode roughshod over the sacred claims of "Christian private and family life" and the rights of the Church bestowed on it by God.[26]

The true ideal was the very opposite; it was the Christian, "organic" state. Just as an organism consists of cells that are combined into a living whole dependent on them while they are dependent on it, so the organic state, according to Schlegel, consisted of "minor centers" forming a living whole around the major center, the monarch. These minor centers—the basis and substance of the state—are the "corporations," i.e., the Family, the Church (fully realized only in its Catholic form), the Guilds (comprising the trades, business, and industry), and the School (comprising the world of learning, education, and science): "This theory of the eternal and essential, original corporations, the Church and the School, the Family and the Guild throws the best, and indeed the only proper, light on the nature and the purpose of the State, if these are to be taken and understood in a positive sense."[27]

This concept of the state, Schlegel insisted, was totally different from the purely negative concept according to which its sole purpose was to safeguard "property and persons." Insofar as the state could be regarded independently of its "natural organs," the corporations, its role was indeed only the maintenance of "external peace," while "inner and spiritual peace" was to be maintained by the Church. In fact, Schlegel laid down that it was best to "govern as little as possible" (though to govern decisively when necessary). Moreover, such a state was essentially conservative; for it was one of its basic principles to "allow continued existence and the maintenance of its legitimate possessions to everything that exists already."[28] Yet, through the corporations, the state had a clearly defined positive function as well; for, while constitutional monarchies on the British pattern had a king who was a ruler in name only, so that they were the battleground of party strife, the government of an organic state would have a genuine monarch with real and very substantial powers. It could, consequently, be above the parties, which it ought to "ignore completely, . . . leave to their own nullity and regard as non-existent," while the monarch—the "principal support, solid center and coping-stone of the whole"—performed an essential role in keeping the powers of the separate corporations in check, maintaining their balance, and ensuring their "living harmony and co-operation." [29]

Evidently, Schlegel no longer quite adhered to the views he had proclaimed in his Vienna lectures on history and literature. The concept of the ethnic state, which, in spite of his federalist views, had been so important to him during the Napoleonic wars, had by now receded into the background. In fact, he now deplored the "national hatred" and the "unlimited national vanity" displayed by so many nations during the last two decades and cherished the fond hope that the days of chauvinism were over.[30] Moreover, throughout the "Signatur des Zeitalters" and in the most marked contrast to his lectures of 1810, he almost studiously avoided comment on the role the nobility was to play in his ideal state. But his basic model was still, as it had been for so many years, the Holy Roman Empire: "Perhaps never in the whole course of world history," he now wrote, "had a greater, organically more comprehensive, free idea of comparable vitality been realized in political life than the idea of the old German Christian Catholic empire as it existed . . . from King Conrad I to Charles V." [31] To sum up, then, however vigorously he himself might have protested against this way of putting it, the way forward for Schlegel was still, or once again, the way back into an irretrievable past.

A similar spirit of conservatism and an even greater fusion of theological and political considerations characterize the articles contributed to the *Concordia* by other writers, particularly those by Schlegel's friend Bucholtz and by three major representatives of the final, Catholic stage of the Romantic movement, Franz von Baader, Zacharias Werner, and Adam Müller. Müller, whose writings considerably influenced the historical school of political economy, presented a theory of national finance "systematically set forth on a theological foundation," defending, among other things, and in complete agreement with Schlegel, the institution of feudal servitude. His article provoked readers to complain to Metternich, who bitterly told Gentz "that he was being deserted on all sides, that those on whom he had most relied were straying into eccentric byways, and that he was offered absurd suggestions instead of concrete assistance." [32]

III *The* Collected Works *of 1822–25*

Another project dating from Schlegel's stay in Frankfort that now matured was the publication of his collected works, which appeared in ten volumes from 1822 to 1825. The task of revising his writings for this purpose proved arduous, as Schlegel had changed his mind on many subjects and wished to incorporate convictions he had developed since his conversion into works written from an entirely different point of view. Thus, for example, the "Gespräch über die Poesie" not only underwent numerous minor changes, but was enlarged by a long final section, in which one of the participants in the dialogue, Ludoviko, breaks a lance on behalf of lyrical poetry and presents a new theory of the genres.[33] In this particular instance, it hardly mattered if this addition occasionally contradicted statements made in the body of the work, as the form of the "Gespräch" amply allowed for the presentation of conflicting points of view.

In other works, the process of revision led to less fortunate results, and the versions of 1822–25 tend to be less consistent than the original publications. They are also far more prolix. Thus, Schlegel's lectures on the history of literature, which had been published in 1815 largely as they had been delivered three years previously, were reissued with the addition of long-winded excursions on the philosophy of language, the Old Testament, and the interpretation of the Scriptures. Nonetheless, the versions of 1822–25 are of considerable interest. Not infrequently, passages that had been ambiguous or obscure in the original publications were now rewritten with greater clarity; very often, indeed, the reader is struck by the extent to which Schlegel succeeded in adapting his early views to his present purposes and incorporating them into his Christian philosophy.

IV *Schlegel's Philosophy of Life*

Schlegel had originally projected "eighteen to twenty volumes"[34] rather than the ten that actually appeared, and was bitterly disappointed when Jacob Mayer & Co., the firm that published his *Sämtliche Werke*, broke up and the enterprise had to be discontinued. He once again surrendered to despondency, until, early in 1826, Christine von Stransky's and his own mystical experiences convinced him that a major crisis in world history was imminent and that this was no time to be idle. The seven years from 1826 to 1833, he was now persuaded,[35] were to be years of a "divine catastrophe," for Christendom must be "smitten down" before it could rise to its full glory; hence, he concluded, it was his duty, as far as lay within his power, to help to prepare mankind for this time of judgment. "One must wake people," he wrote to Christine on April 10, 1827, "wake them mightily, quickly, and repeatedly; but God will also wake them in a terrible fashion. I believe that this will happen very soon and that the time of great terror will begin on Ascension Day." [36]

Soon after he first began to surmise that a time of judgment was at hand, he started to plan a series of lectures on "Christian Philosophy." [37] The more seriously he entertained this project, the more his health of body and mind was restored to him, and for once he achieved more, not less, than he had originally envisaged. During the last two years of his life, he gave three series of public lectures: *Philosophie des Lebens,* delivered in Vienna from March 26 to May 31, 1827; *Philosophie der Geschichte,* Vienna, March 31 to May 30, 1828; and *Philosophie der Sprache und des Wortes,* Dresden, December 12, 1828, to a day or two before his death on January 12, 1829. As these works, which represent the final stage of Schlegel's development as a thinker, overlap in their subject matter and are all based on the same set of ideas, we shall discuss them together.

As Schlegel himself emphasized, his three series of lectures were not systematic in their arrangement. He had always had doubts about philosophic systems, and these doubts had gradually turned into the certainty that all philosophy *more geometrico* was an absurdity. The essential point here is that the dominant systems of his time, those of Fichte and Hegel, were, like that of Spinoza, based on deductive reasoning and on the belief in the supremacy of Reason—a belief well illustrated by Fichte's notorious remark to Schlegel that he would rather spend his time "counting peas" than studying history.[38] Now as early as 1798 Schlegel began to feel that this belief was unwarranted, and that the "vulgar opinion" according to which "the Understanding is more than Reason" was the right one.[39] Consequently, he came to feel that the Fichtean method, which he had so greatly admired in his youth, was futile. He makes this point clearly, if not succinctly, in his *Philosophie der Sprache:*

In the latest period of German philosophy, productive paths of investigation have been explored here and there . . . but on the whole, a pure and abstract mode of thinking that is totally divorced from life is still considered to be the only proper method of philosophy, and is indeed altogether identified with philosophy. This so-called pure and abstract thinking admits no presupposition, is founded on no presupposition, and indeed has no foundation whatever except [that which it creates] itself; starting from itself alone, it has no proper beginning and, for the same reason, no end or aim, but perpetually revolves around itself, within itself, and in its own charmed circle. Now if philosophy moves entirely within this narrow range of thought, and if the art of dialectic exposition is limited to it, but is couched in a language that . . . has at least the merits of lucidity and distinctness . . . , then these exercises in dialectics might very well lead to a fruitful result, if only to a negative one: to the result that the truth and genuine knowledge cannot be reached, should not be sought, and will not be found in this way, and that all this preparatory dialectic exercise in its entirety is nothing more than a mere exercise, that at most can serve but as a first step and an introduction to another manner of fruitful thought, which is in closer touch with life . . .[40]

The idol of all absolute rationalism, according to Schlegel, was a "deadly spirit of absolute negation"; hence, whatever these rational systems predicated of the divine applied in fact less to God than, on the contrary, to the "primal and greatest antagonist of eternal love." [41] Trapped in the maze of their own abstractions, these systems were "dead," and it was in contrast to them that Schlegel called his own philosophy a *Philosophie des Lebens*—a philosophy based not on abstract deductions, but on living experience. Genuine philosophy and theology, he averred, were empirical sciences.[42]

Needless to say, this does not mean that Schlegel had been won over to the side of his lifelong enemy, the empiricism of such thinkers as Locke, Hume, or Condillac; his opposition to their (as it seemed to him) reckless sensationalism was no less radical than his rejection of rationalism:

The first and, indeed, the only way which foreign philosophy took [in its endeavor to oppose rationalism] was to reduce everything to sensation as opposed to reason, and to derive everything from the senses alone, as if reason were merely a secondary faculty, no original power, and ultimately nothing but a sort of chemical precipitate and residuum from the material impressions. But however much may be conceded to these impressions and the external senses . . . , it is still evident that the perception of these sensual impressions, the inner coherence—in short, the unity of consciousness in which they are collected—can never, as indeed has often been objected by the opponents [of sensationalism], have come into the mind from without. . . . This was not, however, the end to which this doctrine had been designed. Rather, the result to which they hoped to come with the aid of this premise was simply the negation of the suprasensible. Whatever in any degree transcends the material impression or sensuous experience, as well as all possible knowledge of and faith in it . . . , absolutely whatever is noble, beautiful, and great, whatever can lead the mind to, or can be referred to, a something suprasensible and divine—all this, wherever it may be found, whether in life or thought, in history or in nature and even in art, it was the object of this philosophy to decry, to involve in doubt, to attack and to overthrow, and to drag everything down to the level of the common and material, or to plunge it into the skeptical abyss of absolute unbelief.[43]

Schlegel's effort at discrediting the empiricists by imputing impure motives to them cannot be justified. If we have quoted this long and involved passage nonetheless, this was because it highlights a basic difference between him and them. While the empiricists started with a minimum of assumptions and mostly arrived— whether to their delight or dismay is beside the point—at a denial of positive religion, Schlegel's philosophy, as he freely admitted, presupposed a positive religion. To attempt to deduce religious truths from philosophy, he was persuaded, was to put the cart before the horse. In the ultimate analysis, philosophy was not, as it was generally held to be, the queen of sciences, but "applied theology." [44] Belief in God was the foundation of all true philosophy, but was not *mere* belief; rather—as Schlegel emphasized, particularly in his repeated efforts at distinguishing his views from those of Jacobi—it was itself a form of empirical knowledge, though one based on kinds of evidence denied or ignored by such thinkers as Condillac.

As Schlegel distinguished between theology and philosophy and tried not to become too deeply involved with the former, his discussion of this evidence is disappointingly brief. In fact, it amounts to little more than the repeated assertion that there are four sources of our knowledge of God, all of an empirical nature: Revelation, the testimony of which is preserved above all in the

Scriptures; Nature, which is a "eulogy of the omnipotence of its Creator"; the voice of Conscience, which has God as its source and origin; and History, which reveals the workings of divine providence.[45] Needless to say, these are thoroughly traditional arguments, and Schlegel claimed no originality on their behalf. Where he felt that he was breaking new ground was in the philosophy he strove to erect on these theological foundations, though here again he attempted to base his arguments on empirical evidence and made ample use of a long tradition of Christian thought.

It is an empirical fact, Schlegel asserts in his *Philosophie des Lebens*, that man's nature is threefold, consisting of Spirit, Soul, and Body; and "this threefold principle is the simple basis of the whole of philosophy." [46] It is reflected throughout life and provides an essential principle of order. Thus, for example, man's "basic feelings of the divine"—faith, hope, and love—are associated, respectively, with spirit, soul, and body. A similar classification applies to the sense organs, sight being associated with the spirit, hearing with the soul, and the lower, "material" senses with the body. In the structure of languages, the vowels correspond to the soul, the consonants to the body, and the spirants to the spirit. In the arts, the threefold division of spirit, soul, and body is reflected in the specific functions of painting, music, and sculpture. Sculpture, being the most physical art, flourished above all among the ancients, while the most spiritual art, painting, rose to its greatest heights in the service of Christianity. Poetry "comprehends and incorporates in itself" the other three arts and also reflects the threefold nature of man. Myth, and consequently the epic, is "the soul of poetry, where spiritual significance and vivid representation completely interpenetrate each other." "Spiritual poems," i.e., direct expressions of faith and the love of God, can hardly be other than lyrical. The more "material" poetry that depends on the "representation of external objects, of events, characters, actions, passions . . . and of historical reality" is associated with the body; this kind of poetry is the special prerogative of the drama and the *Roman*.[47]

Having set up the distinction of body, soul, and spirit, Schlegel reaches a crucial point of his system when he more closely discusses the last two, which together make up human consciousness. A simple act of introspection, he maintains, will show that the soul and the spirit are not simples, but are each, in turn, rent by a dichotomy. Within the soul, imagination and reason are in constant conflict; within the spirit, the will and the understanding wage incessant war.

The classification according to which imagination and reason are ascribed to the soul, while the will and the understanding are assigned to the spirit, may strike the reader as arbitrary; but this is not a matter which is vital to Schlegel's central argument. What is of central importance is his conviction that introspection—i.e., "inner" empirical evidence—shows man's consciousness to be divided into four constituents, whose nature can be further investigated. Man's understanding, he explains, is imperfect, and has to be aided in its tasks by the faculty of reason. Perfect understanding would, however, directly and concretely comprehend the objects of its thought and, hence, require no such assistance. It follows that a being endowed with perfect understanding had no need of reason, so that reason is not a faculty that can be ascribed to God. As similar considerations show, the same can be said of the imagination. Hence, while human consciousness has four constituents, only two of these—will and understanding—can be predicated of God. Now since God has created man in His image, it follows that man cannot *originally* have possessed his present fourfold, divided consciousness. Rather, this divided consciousness is the result of a deterioration that first set in with the Fall of Man and has vitiated human thought and action ever since.

It is worth noting that this theory has a long history in Schlegel's thought and can be traced back all the way to his personal problems as a young man. As will be remembered, it had been his constant complaint, in his earliest extant letters, that his own personality was unbalanced and unduly dominated by the understanding. Subsequently, as we have seen, he had found a similar imbalance and a similar dissociation of the faculties to be a characteristic of the modern, "artificial" civilization as a whole, and had advocated a synthesis of science and art, of philosophy and poetry, of reason and imagination, that would restore the primeval harmony still to be found with the Greeks.

As early as 1799, he had singled out religion as the core and focus of such a synthesis. It is characteristic of the consistency of Schlegel's development that now, some thirty years later, he could still draw on these early problems and aspirations and incorporate them in his Catholic philosophy. In fact, just as, in 1795, he had projected his own psychological difficulties into the world around him and used them to provide an explanation for the nature of the whole development of post-classical art, so he now saw in his theory of the fourfold division of consciousness the key to our understanding of the modern world and the nature of man:

> One of the principal errors of ordinary philosophy, and the principal reason that has prevented it from accomplishing its ends, is the supposition it so hastily admits that the consciousness of man, now entirely changed, broken, mutilated and quartered [*gevierteilt*], is the same as it was originally, and as it was created and fashioned by its Maker; without observing that since the great primeval Revolution, man has not only been outwardly and historically disunited, but even internally and psychologically deranged. The moral being of man, a prey to internal discord, may be said to be quartered, because the four primary faculties of the soul and the spirit of man—Understanding and Will, Reason and Imagination—stand in twofold opposition one to the other . . . Reason in man is the regulating faculty of thought; and in this respect it occupies the first place in life . . . ; but it is unproductive in itself, and even in science it can pretend to no real fertility or immediate intuition. Imagination is fertile and inventive, but left to itself and without guidance, it is blind and hence subject to illusion. The best will, devoid of discernment and understanding, can accomplish little good. Still less capable of good is a strong, and even the strongest, understanding when coupled with a wicked and corrupt character, or an unsteady and changeable will. . . .[48]

This division of consciousness, as a result of which men permit their thoughts and actions to be swayed by one of the four faculties in isolation, is the primary cause of self-deception and error. All human life since the Fall shows the evidence of this flaw. It is at work throughout world history; the four most significant civilizations of the earliest chapter in the story of man, China, India, Egypt, and Israel, were dominated, respectively, by reason, imagination, understanding, and will. In more recent times, the Greeks, the Romans, medieval Europe, and modern Europe from about 1500 onward were successively characterized by the predominance of the understanding, will, imagination, and reason.[49] The same division of consciousness is reflected in recent German philosophy, which, in the systems of Kant, Jacobi, Fichte, and Schelling, has passed through the complete cycle and thus, as it were, erected a monument to each of the four one-sided and, hence, erroneous manners of thinking.[50] (Hegel's system, it seemed to Schlegel, was merely an absurd and pernicious elaboration of Fichtean principles. The hatred and contempt Schlegel felt for Hegel was fully reciprocated by the latter.[51]) But once the flaw in human nature had been recognized and rightly understood, the remedy was within reach: as man's turning away from God had been the cause of the deterioration of consciousness, so man's return to Him would be the cure. As Schlegel repeats in his lectures, though with far greater caution and restraint than in his private letters, a time of judgment was at hand. This judgment would prepare the way for the final stage in the history of mankind, when the unity of consciousness would be restored.

The theory just summarized was probably the main, but by no means Schlegel's sole concern in these lectures. In the *Philosophie des Lebens* and the *Philosophie der Sprache*, he spoke at length about the institution of marriage, the "divine order of nature," the relationship of faith and knowledge, the Christian concept of the state and of law, the struggle between belief and unbelief in his own times, the proper methods of investigation in theology, and a number of related topics. It was plainly his object to show that there was no facet of life upon which a Christian point of view did not shed light, and on many of these facets, he fully agreed with, and therefore reiterated, views deeply rooted in Catholic tradition.

His *Philosophie der Geschichte* is primarily a survey history of the world, emphasizing the history of thought, religion, and political institutions rather than that of battles, conquests, and day-to-day politics. As he explained to Christine von Stransky, these lectures were intended to be "like an Egyptian judgment of the dead concerning all perished nations and empires, as well as those now maturing towards their perdition—a judgment embracing the whole of history from the beginning to the end." The lectures were to "emphasize primarily the seed of inner life and light [*Lebens- und Lichtkern*] in every nation," and to demonstrate how each nation "preserved this seed in its share of the eternal word of God, how it withered and shed its blossom, or how it can still grow to bear the fruit of eternal life." [52]

The quality of this "revue of nations," [53] as Schlegel called it, is uneven; thus, for example, he displays a strong bias against the

Chinese civilization, perhaps because the Chinese sages had for so long been the favorites of the *philosophes*. On the other hand, he was careful not to offend Protestant opinion. While he referred, in a private letter, to Cain, Buddha, Mohammed, and Luther as successive manifestations—"*Stufen*"—of the Antichrist,[54] he went out of his way to do justice to Luther in his public utterances. The breadth of his knowledge in these lectures is as impressive as ever, but his opinions had begun to harden. For instance, he still insisted—and now, in 1828, plainly in the face of all the evidence that had become available in the last twenty years—that the Pentateuch was the "oldest document of the human race";[55] and he speculated more wildly than ever on the origin of languages: "As long as the internal harmony of the soul was undisturbed and unbroken, and the light of the mind still unclouded," he claims, "language could be nothing but the simple beautiful copy or expression of internal lucidity; and, consequently, there could be only one single language. But after the internal word, which had been communicated to man, had become obscured and man's connection with God had been broken, external language was bound to fall into disorder and confusion." [56]

As a result, we are told, there are now three types of languages. Those that have mainly monosyllabic roots and only the rudiments of grammar, like Chinese, are in the overwhelming majority, and form, as it were, the bottom of the pyramid of language. The second type, represented mainly by the Indo-European languages, has predominantly disyllabic roots and a very complex grammatical structure. The top of the pyramid is represented by the Semitic languages, which are supposed to have trisyllabic roots and to be particularly suited to the communication of "prophetic enthusiasm." [57]

Similarly reckless speculations occur throughout the three series of lectures, particularly whenever Schlegel wished to provide evidence for the literal truth of the historical parts of Genesis. Thus, he attempted to disprove the theory of the natural, evolutionary origin of man by asserting that "the possible contagion and communication of various diseases . . . would prove in man rather a greater sympathy and affinity . . . with the cow, the sheep, the camel, the horse, and the elephant, than with the ape," and that "even in the venomous serpent and the mad dog, this deadly affinity of blood . . . exists in a quite different and closer degree, than have yet been discovered in the ape." [58] Or again, he maintained that it "could hardly be doubted" that man had not only been "of a gigantic build" before the Flood, but had been endowed with proportionate spiritual powers; as it could furthermore be assumed that "the air must, in primitive times, have been far more pure and balsamic, and more vital and more nutritive, than at present," the long life of the patriarchs was not to be wondered at. The age Enoch reached, moreover, was particularly significant, not merely because his life spanned as many years as the year has days, but because "in the number of 365 years the number 33 is comprised as a root—a number which, in every respect, and in the most various application, is discovered to be the primary number of the earth. For, with the slight difference of a unit, the number of 365 years corresponds to the sum of 333 plus 33, while the number of days strictly comprised in those 365 years amounts to $4 \times 33,000$ plus 4×330." [59]

It would hardly be fair to Schlegel, however, to dwell on such extravaganzas, or to judge the achievement of the final years of his life in their light. After a century of Hegelianism, Schlegel's conviction that purely deductive philosophical systems devoid of any contact with empirical data cannot be sound is now widely shared, as is his view that philosophies are rarely, if ever, the outcome of purely intellectual activity, but reflect a thinker's total experience of life. It is probably this emphasis on the total, personal experience of the individual believer and his personal relationship with God through prayer and devotion that has stood the test of time best. This emphasis was, of course, not new; the whole Pietist movement—to mention only one example—was founded on it; but Schlegel's attempt to provide this approach to theology with a philosophic basis was a valuable corrective at a time when the main trend was toward ever more abstract systems and secured him a position of considerable importance among the Catholic thinkers of his day.[60] Strangely enough, however, Schlegel's lectures of 1827–29 seem to have reached a wider public in England than in predominantly Catholic countries. In the German original, the three series of lectures, which first appeared in rapid succession in 1828–30, were reissued as part of the second edition of Schlegel's *Collected Works* in 1846, but—perhaps because this second edition was fairly large—were never afterward reprinted.[61] The French translations of the *Philosophie der Geschichte* (1836) and the *Philosophie des Lebens* (1838) never saw a second edition. The English version of the *Philosophie der Geschichte,* on the other hand, was brought out in six successive editions between 1835 and 1852 and reprinted once again in 1888.

Friedrich Schlegel spent the evening of January 11, 1829, with his old friend, Ludwig Tieck, at the house of a common acquaintance. Around 11 P.M. he returned to his study in the house of his niece, Auguste von Butlar, to resume work on the tenth lecture of his *Philosophie der Sprache.* There, at his desk, and pen in hand—he had just commenced a sentence about that "entirely perfect and complete understanding" [62] for which he had striven throughout his life—he suffered a stroke, and a few hours later, he expired in the arms of his niece.[63]

His old enemies promptly circulated the rumor that he had choked to death on a dish of *pâté de foie gras*[64]—a gratuitous insult to the memory of the deceased that would not be worth mentioning if it had not been an omen of things to come. Within a few years of Schlegel's death, the intellectual atmosphere in Germany underwent a radical change, and a vigorous reaction against the Romantic outlook set in. Among all the leaders of the Romantic movement, Schlegel was the most obvious target for attacks.

There can be no doubt that the reaction of the 1830's against Romanticism can, to a certain extent, be justified. However greatly we may admire the literary criticism of a Schlegel, the lyrical poetry of a Brentano, or the daring speculations of a Novalis, it cannot be denied that the Romantic movement had turned into an impediment in the way toward social progress and political liberty. The Romantics' preference for the free play of the imagination, for symbolism, and for the cultivation of Germany's medieval heritage militated against the serious and effective investigation, in works of art, of the pressing sociological problems of the time. Romantic politics provided support for those privileged by birth and possessions, for censorship and political repression, for every conceivable attempt at turning the clock back or at least preventing it from keeping time; and Romantic religion—despite such individual actions as Brentano's contributions to charities—was at a considerable remove from Christ's concern for the dispossessed.

But the attacks that were heaped on Schlegel's memory were all too rarely of a factual, objective kind, and consisted mainly of a tissue of misunderstandings, insinuations, and errors. Had he not commenced his literary activities by being insolent to his betters, such as Schiller, and continued them by making a public display of his own licentiousness? Had he not betrayed the ideals of his youth by becoming a Catholic, and had he not abetted that "Prince of Darkness," Metternich? Had his conversion not made him lazy and hypocritical—or rather, had he not always been lazy and added insult to injury by inserting in his pornographic novel a hymn to sloth? His stock was sinking low indeed, and this at a time when countless philologists, literary critics, and historians of literature were—largely without being aware of it—continuing investigations he had started with the aid of intellectual tools he had fashioned or refined.

In the end, however, the emphasis on the history of literature which he had done so much to foster came to his rescue. In 1870, Rudolf Haym wrote his monumental study of the Romantic school —a book that was inspired by a profound dislike of many aspects of Romanticism, but which demonstrated, once and for all, that this movement, whatever its merits or demerits may be, would never have attained its historical significance without Friedrich Schlegel. In 1882, Jacob Minor made his early writings, which had become rarities in their original form, easily available again; and ever since, the young Schlegel has been recognized as one of the great seminal minds of his age and as—to quote René Wellek— "one of the greatest critics of history." [65] As regards his later writings, it was not until the 1920's, when Josef Körner discovered a part of his notebooks, published his correspondence, and demonstrated the continuity of his development, that they became, once again, the object of serious study. In recent years, further, and very extensive, manuscripts have come to light, whose riches have as yet hardly been skimmed, and which strongly suggest that Schlegel's role in the history of German philosophic Idealism has been underrated. His early criticism is now read more widely than at any time in the last one hundred and fifty years. How much significance for our days the work of his later phase possesses, only the future will show.

Notes and References

The abbreviations used in references to Schlegel's writings and to his correspondence (italicized even if they are editor's names) are explained in the bibliography under Primary Sources (Sections A–D). Works on Schlegel listed under Secondary Sources are referred to by the name of the author only, or—if this is necessary to avoid ambiguity—by the author's name and the year of publication.

In accordance with the general practice, Schlegel's "Fragmente" are referred to by the numbers given them in Minor's edition of the *Prosaische Jugendschriften* and repeated in the *Kritische Friedrich-Schlegel-Ausgabe*, the abbreviations used being *Lyc. F.* for the "Lyceums-Fragmente" (*KA*, II, 147–63) and *Ath. F.* for the "Athenäums-Fragmente" (*KA*, II, 165–255). The same method is used with the "Ideen" (*KA*, II, 256–72).

Preface

1. Ernst Behler's brilliant biography in the series *rowohlts monographien* was written with the same need for compression as my own book.

Chapter One

1. Throughout this book, the word "romantic" and its cognates are capitalized when, and only when, reference is made to people, events, styles, etc., within the German Romantic movement.

2. ". . . Ich liebe nichts, gar niemand. Bedenke was in diesen Worten liegt und preise Dich glücklich, daß Du große Leiden hast!" —"Ich habe Verstand, aber bin so unerfahren, beschränkt, und vor allem—es wäre ungerecht mir die Seele abzusprechen, aber die Seele der Seele, lieber Wilhelm, die fehlt mir doch ganz offenbar, nämlich der Sinn für Liebe."—"Ich weiß, daß ich gar nicht leben kann, wenn ich nicht groß bin, d. h. mit mir zufrieden. Denn mein Verstand ist so, daß wäre alles ihm gleich, und Harmonie in mir, so wäre ichs schon." (*Walzel, Briefe*, pp. 17, 108, 94.)

3. *Ibid.*, pp. 58, 68.

4. "Ich sehe die offenbare Unmöglichkeit ein, mich itzt in ein bürgerliches Joch zu schmiegen . . . Ich brauche Dir nun schon nicht zu sagen, welches mein Ziel ist; zu leben, *frei* zu leben . . . Du kennst mich nun schon so lange—denke noch einmal über mich nach, und sage mir, wozu ich bestimmt bin, was aus mir werden wird, was ich tun soll?" (*Ibid.*, p. 90; cf. p. 94.)

5. *DNL 143*, pp. 245–69.

6. *Minor*, I, 77–178.

7. For more detailed treatments of this topic, see E. M. Butler, *The Tyranny of Greece over Germany* (Cambridge, England, 1935); W. Rehm, *Griechentum und Goethezeit* (Leipzig, 1936); Henry Hatfield, *Aesthetic Paganism in German Literature* (Cambridge, Mass., 1964). Radically different views had been proposed by Herder and other writers of the Storm-and-Stress movement as early as 1770; but though this movement, in many ways, prepared the ground for the Romantics, it did not win out over the Enlightenment, and its work had to be done all over again.

8. Notebook "Zur Philologie," *Logos*, XVII (1928), 16.

9. "Die Natur aber und das Gebäude der schönsten Körper ist selten ohne Mängel . . . Dieser Erfahrung gemäß verfuhren diese weisen Künstler, wie ein geschickter Gärtner, welcher verschiedene Absenker von edlen Arten auf einen Stamm propfet; und wie eine Biene aus vielen Blumen sammlet, so blieben die Begriffe der Schönheit nicht auf das Individuelle einzelne Schöne eingeschränkt, wie es zuweilen die Begriffe der alten und neuern Dichter, und der mehresten heutigen Künstler sind, sondern sie suchten das Schöne aus vielen schönen Körpern zu vereinigen. Sie reinigten ihre Bilder von aller persönlichen Neigung, welche unsern Geist von dem wahren Schönen abziehet." (J. J. Winckelmann, *Geschichte der Kunst des Altertums*, Dresden, 1764, p. 154.)

10. J. J. Winckelmann, *Gedanken über die Nachahmung der griechischen Werke in der Malerei und Bildhauerkunst*, 2nd ed. (Dresden, 1786), p. 3.

11. C. H. Heydenreich, *System der Ästhetik*, I (Leipzig, 1790), 26.

12. Rehm, *op. cit.* (above, note 7), p. 61. Christopher Lloyd, "The Noble Savage," *The Listener*, 13 November 1952, pp. 814f.

13. Cf., e.g., Heydenreich, *op. cit.*, I, 30; F. Bouterwek, *Parallelen. Vom griechischen und modernen Genius. Nur Fragmente* (Göttingen, 1791), pp. 14, 17f.

14. See Immanuel Kant, *Ideen zu einer allgemeinen Geschichte in weltbürgerlicher Absicht* (1784) and *Mutmaßlicher Anfang des Menschengeschlechts* (1786).

15. "Die Geschichte der griechischen Dichtkunst ist eine allgemeine Naturgeschichte der Dichtkunst; eine vollkommne und gesetzgebende

Anschauung." "Die griechische Poesie in Masse ist ein *Maximum und Kanon der natürlichen Poesie,* und auch jedes einzelne Erzeugnis derselben ist das vollkommenste in seiner Art." (*Minor,* I, 125, 145.)

16. The adjective Schlegel uses is "*interessant,*" which would normally be translated as "interesting" rather than "interested"; the latter rendering, however, seems to be closer to Schlegel's meaning.

17. *Minor,* I, 92.

18. *Minor,* I, 91.

19. "Die Philosophie poetisiert und die Poesie philosophiert: die Geschichte wird als Dichtung, diese aber als Geschichte behandelt. Selbst die Dichtarten verwechseln gegenseitig ihre Bestimmung; eine lyrische Stimmung wird Gegenstand eines Drama, und ein dramatischer Stoff wird in lyrische Form gezwängt." (*Minor,* I, 89.)

20. Cf. his notebooks "Von der Schönheit in der Dichtkunst" (*N.ph. Sch.,* pp. 363–87).

21. *Minor,* I, 106f., 142. Schiller pointed out that Jocasta's suicide and Oedipus' self-mutilation can hardly be called a harmonious resolution of a conflict. Schlegel might well have replied that *Oedipus Rex* was not intended as a tale of horrors, but as a vindication of the Delphic oracle and the power of the gods, and that, in any case, Sophocles' last word on the subject of Oedipus was not *Oedipus Rex,* but *Oedipus at Colonus.* Cf. *KA,* VI, 283 and p. 121 below.

22. Cf. H. W. Ziegler, "F. Schlegels Jugendentwicklung," *Archiv für die gesamte Psychologie,* LX (1927), 1–128.

Chapter Two

1. Cf. Brinkmann, *passim.*

2. Cf. Eichner (1955), *passim.* The periodical *Die Horen,* in which Schiller's treatise was published, ran about one month behind schedule.

3. Cf. Walzel's review of Carl Alt, *Schiller und die Brüder Schlegel* in *Euphorion,* XII, 193–217, and A. Garreau, *Saint-Empire* (Paris, 1954), p. 122.

4. *Walzel, Briefe,* p. 253.

5. *Minor,* I, 79, 83.

6. More detailed accounts will be found in Rouge (1904), Körner (1924), and *KA,* II.

7. For a thorough account, see Wellek, vols. I and II.

8. *The Works of Shakespeare,* ed. A. Pope (London, 1725), I, xxiii.

9. Cf. Haym, pp. 165–76.

10. Quoted from Haym, p. 169.

11. W. v. Humboldt to Jacobi, January 23, 1797. (O. Fambach, *Ein Jahrhundert deutscher Literaturkritik,* 5 vols., Berlin, 1957ff., II, 346f. Cf. *ibid.,* IV, 69ff.)

12. There is of course no contradiction between this assertion and

Schlegel's treatment of Jacobi. He had examined Jacobi's published works, not snooped into his private affairs.

13. *N.ph.Sch.*, pp. 363–87.

14. *Minor*, I, 138f.; *LN*, 1569, and the comment on this note, *ibid.*, p. 277.

15. "The longer the story, consistently with its being comprehensible as a whole, the finer it is by reason of its magnitude." (*Poetics*, Ch. 7; Bywater's translation.)

16. "Durch sie [die Göttlichkeit] ist eine Schönheit das *Bild der Gottheit, die Kunst ihre Sprache*. Der Künstler ein wahrer Sprecher Gottes." "*Die Göttlichkeit* (Erscheinung der Allheit) ist der *herrschende*, höchste, königliche *Teil des Schönen*. (*N.ph.Sch.*, pp. 376, 377.)

17. *Walzel, Briefe*, p. 110.

18. *N.ph.Sch.*, p. 364.

19. *LN*, 1733, 1135.

20. *KA*, II, 91.

21. *KA*, II, 14.

22. "Der reine Ästhetiker sagt, so *liebe* ich das Gedicht, der reine Philosoph, so *verstehe* ichs. Die Frage vom *Wert* ist ursprünglich schon ethisch." (*LN*, 1044).

23. "Alle eigentlichen ästhetischen Urteile sind ihrer Natur nach *Machtsprüche* und können nichts andres sein. Beweisen kann man sie nicht, legitimieren aber muß man sich dazu." (*LN*, 71.)

24. *Lyc. F.*, 57. Cf. Wellek, II, 10.

25. *LN*, 14, 999, 1779.

26. Preface to *Dorian Gray*.

27. Quoted from John Dewey, *Art as Experience* (New York, 1934), p. 304.

28. Cf. *KA*, II, 101f.

29. "Wie viele gibt es denn wohl, welche, auch nachdem der Reiz der Neuheit ganz vorüber ist, zu einer Schrift, die es verdient, immer von neuem zurückkehren können; nicht um die Zeit zu töten, noch um Kenntnisse von dieser oder jener Sache zu erwerben, sondern um sich den Eindruck durch die Wiederholung schärfer zu bestimmen, und um sich das Beste ganz anzueignen? So lange es daran fehlt, muß ein reifes Urteil über geschriebene Kunstwerke unter die seltensten Seltenheiten gehören." (*KA*, II, 79.)

30. "Man sollte sich ordentlich kunstmäßig üben, eben sowohl äußerst langsam mit steter Zergliederung des Einzelnen, als auch schneller und in einem Zuge zur Übersicht des Ganzen lesen zu können. Wer nicht beides kann, und jedes anwendet, wo es hingehört, der weiß eigentlich noch gar nicht zu lesen." (*KA*, II, 84.)

31. *Lyc. F.*, 27 (R. Wellek's translation, Wellek, II, 8).

32. "Ebenso widersinnig ist es, wenn man ohne Vorkenntnis der einzelnen Schrift eines Autors rezensierend zu Leibe geht, für den, vielleicht eben darum, weil er Charakter hat, nur durch wiederholtes Studium aller seiner . . . Werke, der eigentliche Gesichtspunkt gefunden werden kann, auf den doch alles ankommt." (*KA*, II, 90.)

33. *LN*, 72.

34. *Lessing*, I, 23.

35. *Minor*, I, 309; cf. Wellek, II, 10. For a less optimistic view expressed by Schlegel, see *KA*, II, 349.

36. "Der Unterschied der Poesie und der Prosa besteht darin, daß die Poesie darstellen, die Prosa nur mitteilen will." (*Lessing*, I, 7.)

37. *Lyc. F.*, 117.

38. Cf. *LN*, 518, 579, 622, 792, 808, 1566; *Ath. F.*, 238, 247.

39. *Walzel, Briefe*, p. 173. There is an obvious slip of the pen in the original passage: Schlegel wrote "Geschichte der Ästhetik" instead of "Geschichte der Poesie." Cf. *N.ph.Sch.*, p. 363.

40. *Walzel, Briefe*, p. 360.

41. *KA*, II, 290.

42. *Caroline*, II, 585.

43. *KA*, XIII, 24.

44. *KA*, XII, 420.

45. Ernst Cassirer, *The Philosophy of the Enlightenment*, tr. by F. C. Koelln and J. P. Pettegrove (Boston: Beacon Press, 1955), p. 296; cf. *ibid.*, pp. 6, 23. It need hardly be pointed out that the eighteenth century nonetheless produced excellent historians.

46. Cf. Dilthey (1870), p. 218; Dilthey, "Wilhelm Scherer zum persönlichen Gedächtnis," *Deutsche Rundschau*, IL (1886), 137; Mettler, *passim; KA*, VI, xiff., xxxiff.

Chapter Three

1. Cf. Robson-Scott, pp. 113ff.

2. See pp. 95f. below.

3. *LN*, 920, 1846; *Lyc. F.*, 126; *KA*, XII, 404; *Ath. F.*, 82; *Lyc. F.*, 9. It should be noted that in the eighteenth century German "Witz" corresponded far more closely to English "wit" than it does now. For a more detailed discussion, see *KA*, II, xxxvff.

4. *Characteristics of Men, Manners, Opinions, Times* (5th ed., London, 1732), I, 290.

5. "Es ist gleich tödlich für den Geist, ein System zu haben, und keins zu haben. Er wird sich also wohl entschließen müssen, beides zu verbinden." (*Ath. F.*, 53.)

6. *Walzel, Briefe*, p. 336.

7. "Mein Versuch über das Studium der griechischen Poesie ist ein

manierierter Hymnus in Prosa auf das Objektive in der Poesie. Das Schlechteste daran scheint mir der gänzliche Mangel der unentbehrlichen Ironie; und das Beste, die zuversichtliche Voraussetzung, daß die Poesie unendlich viel wert sei; als ob dies eine ausgemachte Sache wäre."—"Alle klassischen Dichtarten in ihrer strengen Reinheit sind jetzt lächerlich."—"Aus dem, was die Modernen wollen, muß man lernen, was die Poesie werden soll: aus dem, was die Alten tun, was sie sein muß."—"Die Alten sind weder die Juden, noch die Christen, noch die Engländer der Poesie. Sie sind nicht ein willkürlich ausgewähltes Kunstvolk Gottes; noch haben sie den alleinseligmachenden Schönheitsglauben; noch besitzen sie ein Dichtungsmonopol."—"In den Alten sieht man den vollendeten Buchstaben der ganzen Poesie: in den Neuern ahnt man den werdenden Geist." (*Lyc. F.*, 7, 60, 84, 91, 93.)

8. See Eichner (1956), pp. 1019ff.

9. Cf. Ullmann, *KA*, II, liiff., and P. Völker, "Die Bedeutungsentwicklung des Wortes 'Roman'," *Zs. f. romanische Philologie*, X (1886), 485ff. For the use of "romantic" in descriptions of landscapes, etc., see Immerwahr (1960).

10. Johnson, Preface to Father J. Lobo, *A Voyage to Abyssinia* (London, 1735), p. vii.

11. Thus, for example, Wieland called Schiller's *Don Carlos* a "dramatischer Roman," while Schiller said that *Die Räuber* was a "dramatischer Roman" rather than a "theatralisches Drama." Herder called Shakespeare's *Romeo and Juliet* a *Roman* and wrote of "Romane in Shakespeares Manier," A. W. Schlegel called Shakespeare's plays "Romanspiele," and F. Schlegel declared that these plays were "dem Wesen nach *psychologische Romane*." (See *KA*, II, lvii; *KA*, V, lviiif.; Eichner 1956, pp. 1020f.)

12. Thus, A. O. Lovejoy argues that "romantic" in Schlegel's usage cannot have anything to do with *Roman* because Schlegel had called Shakespeare a romantic poet, and Ullmann and Gotthard write of a "ziemlich feststehender Begriff des Romans" (p. 146) which Schlegel is supposed to have "zerpflückt."

13. "Drei herrschende Dichtarten. 1) *Tragödie* bei den Griechen 2) *Satire* bei den Römern 3) *Roman* bei den Modernen." (*LN*, 32.) "Wie der Roman die ganze moderne Poesie, so tingiert auch die Satire . . . die ganze römische Poesie." (*Ath. F.*, 146.) "Wie unsre Dichtkunst mit dem Roman, so fing die der Griechen mit dem Epos an und löste sich wieder drin auf." (*KA*, II, 335.)

14. For evidence, see Eichner (1956), *passim*.

15. *KA*, II, 290–303.

16. *KA*, II, 302.

17. *Ibid*.

18. *KA,* II, 290.
19. *Walzel, Briefe,* p. 170; *KA,* II, 346.
20. *KA,* II, 345, 346.
21. *KA,* II, 347.
22. Cf. *KA,* II, lxxiff.
23. *LN,* 1771; *KA,* II, 336.
24. *LN,* 340.
25. Cf., e.g., *LN,* 4, 20, 55, 79, 120, 185, 582.
26. *KA,* II, 80.
27. *KA* II, 336.
28. *LN,* 1727.
29. See *KA,* II, ciii.
30. *Tristram Shandy,* Bk. I, Ch. 4.
31. *LN,* 2079, 1709. The interlocking of stories is, of course, already to be found in Greek prose romances, such as the *Aethiopics;* but Schlegel himself was always aware that many of the characteristics he called "essentially modern" or "romantic" could be traced back, to some extent, to works written before the fall of the Roman Empire: "Die natürliche und die künstliche ästhetische Bildung greifen ineinander, und die Spätlinge der antiken Poesie sind zugleich die Vorläufer der modernen." (*Minor,* I, 80.)
32. *Schillers Briefe,* ed. Jonas (Stuttgart [1892–96]), III, 245f.; *N.ph.Sch.,* p. 370.
33. *Minor,* I, 13.
34. Cf. *Walzel, Briefe,* pp. 21, 364; *LN,* 1646; *Lyc. F.,* 69, 79, 95, 108.
35. "Verbindet die Extreme, so habt ihr die wahre Mitte." (*KA,* II, 263: *Ideen,* 74.)
36. *Ath. F.,* 116.
37. Milton, *L'Allegro,* line 133; quoted by Schlegel as the "earliest wrong view" of Shakespeare, *LN,* 1150.
38. *LN,* 1961 (my italics).
39. "gebildete Willkür" (*KA,* II, 134).
40. *KA,* II, 318f.
41. *LN,* 1804.
42. See Polheim (1966), *passim.*
43. *LN,* 735. Cf. Eichner (1956), pp. 1024ff.
44. *KA,* II, 285.
45. *LN,* 735.
46. F. Bouterwek, *Geschichte der Künste und Wissenschaften,* I (Göttingen, 1801), 20.
47. *KA,* II, 333. It should be noted in passing that Schiller speaks of "das Sentimentalische," Schlegel (in a somewhat different sense) of "das Sentimentale"; neither uses the noun "Sentimentalität."

48. *LN*, 56.

49. *KA*, II, 333.

50. "Die alte Poesie schließt sich durchgängig an die Mythologie an, und vermeidet sogar den eigentlich historischen Stoff . . . Der Dichter, der eine wahre Begebenheit, die das ganze Volk ernstlich anging, darstellte, ward bestraft. Die romantische Poesie hingegen ruht ganz auf historischem Grunde . . . Das erste beste Schauspiel, das Sie sehn, irgend eine Erzählung die Sie lesen; wenn eine geistreiche Intrige darin ist, können Sie fast mit Gewißheit darauf rechnen, daß wahre Geschichte zum Grunde liegt, wenngleich vielfach umgebildet." (*KA*, II, 334.)

51. For a more detailed discussion of "Fülle" and "Einheit," see Polheim (1966), pp. 56–66. Cf. Behler (1957), pp. 220ff., 229, and *KA*, XVIII, xviff.

52. "χαός und ἔρως ist wohl die beste Erklärung des Romantischen." (*LN*, 1760.)

53. "Nicht der Haß sondern die Liebe sondert das Chaos." (*LN*, 1514.)

54. Cf., e.g., Goethe's letters to Boisserée of November 24, 1831, and to Humboldt of March 17, 1832.

55. *Ath. F.*, 162; *SW*, XV, 52f.

56. *Lyc. F.*, 23.

57. *Lyc. F.*, 37.

58. ". . . Es gibt Künstler, welche nicht etwa zu groß von der Kunst denken, denn das ist unmöglich, aber doch nicht frei genug sind, sich selbst über ihr Höchstes zu erheben." (*Lyc. F.*, 87.)

59. "Wir müssen uns über unsre eigne Liebe erheben, und was wir anbeten, in Gedanken vernichten können; sonst fehlt uns, was wir auch für andre Fähigkeiten haben, der Sinn für das Weltall." (*KA*, II, 131.)

60. *Lyc. F.*, 28; *Ath. F.*, 51. Cf. *LN*, 207.

61. *Lyc. F.*, 108.

62. *Lyc. F.*, 108.

63. *KA*, XVIII, 128 [76].

64. *Lyc. F.*, 42.

65. Cf. Polheim (1966), pp. 103ff.

66. *Lyc. F.*, 108.

67. *Ideen*, 69.

68. Cf. Herman Meyer, *Zarte Empirie: Studien zur Literaturgeschichte* (Stuttgart, 1963), pp. 84, 111. Peter Michelsen, *Laurence Sterne und der deutsche Roman des 18. Jahrhunderts* (Göttingen, 1962). It is no coincidence that Schlegel's preference for novels influenced by Sterne and his interest in irony culminate at nearly the same time.

69. *Walzel, Briefe*, p. 32.

70. *LN*, 506.

71. *LN*, 481.

72. *LN*, 48.

73. The best and most recent accounts are those by Immerwahr (1951), Strohschneider-Kohrs (1960), and Behler (1963a).

74. Wellek, II, 16.

75. For a more detailed account, see Körner's introduction to *N.ph.Sch.*

76. *Walzel, Briefe*, pp. 235f.

77. See H. Butterfield, *The Origins of Modern Science, 1300–1800* (London, 1965), p. 50. A. R. Hall, *The Scientific Revolution, 1500–1800* (London-New York-Toronto, 1954), pp. 149ff., 172.

78. Quoted from Arthur Cobban, *In Search of Humanity; The Role of the Enlightenment in Modern History* (London, 1960), pp. 43f.

79. F. Hemsterhuis, *Lettre sur l'homme et ses rapports*, avec le commentaire inédit de Diderot. Texte établi . . . par G. May (New Haven, 1964), p. 151.

80. *KA*, XVIII, 8 [48], 5 [11], 4 [7], 5 [12].

81. *Minor*, II, 112ff.

82. *Ath. F.*, 216.

83. *N.ph.Sch.*, pp. 126, 147, 156.

84. *KA*, II, 315.

85. *Ideen*, 108; cf. *Lyc. F.*, 115 and *KA*, II, lxxxf.

86. *Über die Religion. Reden an die Gebildeten unter ihren Verächtern* (Berlin, 1799), pp. 50, 53, 55.

87. *Preitz*, p. 130.

88. *KA*, II, 255–72.

89. *Ideen*, 8, 11, 13, 34, 43, 46, 48, 62, 96.

90. *Ideen*, 38.

91. *KA*, II, 313.

92. *KA*, XVIII, 154 [378].

93. *KA*, II, 312.

94. *Ibid.*

95. "Seid der Größe des Zeitalters würdig, und der Nebel wird von Euren Augen sinken . . . Alles Denken ist ein Divinieren, aber der Mensch fängt erst eben an, sich seiner divinatorischen Kraft bewußt zu werden. Welche unermeßliche Erweiterung wird sie noch erfahren; und eben jetzt. Mich däucht wer das Zeitalter, das heißt jenen großen Prozeß allgemeiner Verjüngung, jene Prinzipien der ewigen Revolution verstünde, dem müßte es gelingen können, die Pole der Menschheit zu ergreifen und das Tun der ersten Menschen, wie den Charakter der goldnen Zeit die noch kommen wird, zu erkennen und zu wissen." (*KA*, II, 322.)

96. "In einem gewissen Sinne sind wohl alle Gedichte Romane . . ." (*LN*, 573).

97. "Da suche und finde ich das Romantische, bei den ältern Modernen, bei Shakespeare, Cervantes, in der italiänischen Poesie, in jenem Zeitalter der Ritter, der Liebe und der Märchen, aus welchem die Sache und das Wort selbst herstammt. Dieses ist bis jetzt das einzige, was einen Gegensatz zu den klassischen Dichtungen des Altertums abgeben kann; nur diese ewig frischen Blüten der Fantasie sind würdig die alten Götterbilder zu umkränzen. Und gewiß ist es, daß alles Vorzüglichste der modernen Poesie dem Geist und selbst der Art nach dahinneigt; es müßte denn eine Rückkehr zum Antiken sein sollen. Wie unsre Dichtkunst mit dem Roman, so fing die der Griechen mit dem Epos an und löste sich wieder darin auf. Nur mit dem Unterschiede, daß das Romantische nicht sowohl eine Gattung ist als ein Element der Poesie, das mehr oder minder herrschen und zurücktreten, aber nie ganz fehlen darf. Es muß Ihnen nach meiner Ansicht einleuchtend sein, daß und warum ich fodre, alle Poesie solle romantisch sein; den Roman aber, insofern er eine besondre Gattung sein will, verabscheue." (*KA*, II, 335.)

98. *Ath. F.*, 116.

99. "Ein Roman ist ein romantisches Buch.—Sie werden das für eine nichtssagende Tautologie ausgeben. Aber ich will Sie zuerst nur darauf aufmerksam machen, daß man sich bei einem Buche schon ein Werk, ein für sich bestehendes Ganze denkt. Alsdann liegt ein sehr wichtiger Gegensatz gegen das Schauspiel darin, welches bestimmt ist angeschaut zu werden: der Roman hingegen war es von den ältesten Zeiten für die Lektüre . . . Das Schauspiel soll auch romantisch sein, wie alle Dichtkunst; aber ein Roman ists nur unter gewissen Einschränkungen, <oder um es bestimmter zu sagen, das neuere Drama ist> ein angewandter Roman." (*KA*, II, 335f.; the words in pointed brackets, which remove an awkward ambiguity, were added by Schlegel in 1823.)

Chapter Four

1. *KA*, V, 1–82. For the rest of this chapter, cf. Kluckhohn (*passim*) and *KA*, V, xvii–lxix. For translations of *Lucinde*, see p. 165 below.

2. *F. H. Jacobis auserlesener Briefwechsel* (Leipzig, 1827), II, 175.

3. Polheim (1963), pp. 113–15.

4. Cf. A. W. Schlegel's translation of this poem, *Athenäum*, III (1800), 218–24.

5. *Caroline*, I, 514f.

6. While Schlegel was probably indebted to Novalis for the *motif* of the *Liebestod*, there is an important difference in their treatment of it. With Novalis the lover longs for a mystical reunion in death

after he has lost his beloved. Schlegel's treatment of the *motif* may strike the reader as a little less morbid if its wider implications are realized. The ultimate reason for the death wish is the conviction that everything finite, and hence even the lovers' bliss in each other's arms, is imperfect. Anyone who has the "feeling for the universe" which is the essence of religion will always be tormented by his thirst for the infinite—a thirst that can only be quenched through reunion with God or the Absolute in death. A. W. Schlegel's famous definition, according to which "the poetry of the ancients was that of possession" while "ours is that of longing," is closely connected with this idea.

7. *LN*, 1527.

8. Notebook: "Die meisten Männer sind impotent. Impotenz trennt die Ehe, und so werden weit weniger Ehen gebrochen als man denkt. Wer eine Frau nicht befriedigen kann, ist impotent." (*LN*, 1444.) Novel: "Ein Mann, der das innere Verlangen seiner Geliebten nicht ganz füllen und befriedigen kann, versteht es gar nicht zu sein, was er doch ist und sein soll. Er ist eigentlich unvermögend, und kann keine gültige Ehe schließen." (*KA*, V, 21.)

Chapter Five

1. *Dorothea*, I, 19.

2. *Ibid.*, I, 27.

3. Cf. Josef Körner in *N.ph.Sch.*, pp. 45ff.

4. *KA*, V, 282.

5. *Europa*, I, 1 (1803), p. 60.

6. For the text of *Alarcos* and a more detailed account, see *KA*, V, lxxi–lxxxi, 221–62.

7. *KA*, II, 373–96.

8. Cf. K. K. Polheim, *Novellentheorie und Novellenforschung* (Stuttgart, 1965), pp. 62ff. Benno von Wiese, *Novelle* (Stuttgart, 1963), pp. 13ff.

9. Varnhagen von Ense, *Galerie von Bildnissen aus Rahels Umgang und Briefwechsel* (Leipzig, 1836), I, 231.

10. For the following, cf. Behler (1963b).

11. *KA*, VII, 63.

12. *KA*, VII, 75f.

13. *KA*, VII, 78. The role assigned to India reflects ideas proposed by Herder. The North is associated with magnetism and hence with iron, which played an important role in Romantic pseudo-science.

14. *Europa*, I, 1, p. 45.

15. *KA*, IV, 9–152.

16. *KA*, IV, 79, 93.

17. *KA*, IV, 56, 99f.

18. For a more detailed account, see *KA*, IV, xix–xxx.

19. Cf. *KA*, XI, xxix–xxxvi.

20. *KA*, XI, 159f.

21. *Poetisches Taschenbuch für das Jahr 1806*, pp. 257–390 = *KA*, IV, 153–204. Cf. *KA*, IV, xxxff. and Robson-Scott, pp. 129–45.

22. Robson-Scott, pp. 130, 136, 137.

23. *Briefe an Ludwig Tieck*, ed. K. v. Holtei (Breslau, 1864), p. 329.

24. Willson, p. 212.

25. To assess the importance of Schlegel's insistence on grammatical criteria, his views have to be compared with those of contemporaries like Adelung, who, in 1806, asserted the common origin of Sanskrit, Hebrew, Turkish, Hungarian, etc. on the basis of such similarities as Sanskrit *nâra* (water) and Hebrew *nahar* (river). Cf. Th. Benfey, *Geschichte der Sprachwissenschaft und der orientalischen Philologie in Deutschland* (Munich, 1869), pp. 357ff., and Twadell, *passim*.

26. Willson, p. 217.

27. *Indier*, p. 95.

28. *Ibid.*, pp. 172ff. It should be pointed out, however, that Schlegel's criteria were linguistic rather than racial, that he rarely displayed racial prejudices, and that he did not use the word "Aryan."

29. For a scholarly assessment, see Oppenberg.

30. Cf. Willson, *passim*.

31. "Alle Theologie [ist] Poesie." (*LN*, 1664.) ". . . aber jeder Gott, dessen Vorstellung der Mensch sich nicht *macht* d.h. frei hervorbringt, sondern geben läßt, diese Vorstellung mag übrigens noch so sublimiert sein [ist] ein *Abgott*." (*Minor*, II, 105) "Die Religion ist Sache der Willkür." (*KA*, XVIII, 110 [973].

32. *KA*, VI, 246; cf. *ibid.*, pp. 93, 244 and pp. 134f. below.

33. *KA*, XII, 151.

34. Cf. Josef Körner, *Marginalien* (Frankfurt, 1950), pp. 82f.

35. Cf. K. Joel, *Nietzsche und die Romantik* (Jena, 1923) and W. Kohlschmidt, "Nihilismus der Romantik," *Form und Innerlichkeit* (Bern, 1955), pp. 157ff.

36. *Walzel, Briefe*, p. 501.

37. Körner, *F. u. D.*, pp. 222, 545.

38. *Franz Sternbalds Wanderungen* (1798); Ludwig Tieck's *Schriften* (Berlin, 1828), XVI, 334ff.

39. *Athenäum*, II (1799), 144.

40. *Dorothea*, I, 165f.

41. *KA*, XVIII, p. 398 [925].

42. Notebook *Zur Philosophie*, 1806. II.

43. *Lessing*, II, 11f.

44. *Dorothea*, I, 163.

Chapter Six

1. *Lessing,* III, 409.
2. *Krisenjahre,* I, 270f.
3. *Ibid.,* I, 293.
4. *Über die neuere Geschichte* (*KA,* VII, 125–407). For details, see E. Behler in *KA,* VII, lxxvii–xciii, and Lorenz (*passim*).
5. *Boisserée,* I, 78.
6. *Leipziger Litteratur-Zeitung,* 1812, col. 2621.
7. "Adel also und Freiheit waren die Grundfesten der ältesten deutschen Verfassung . . . Bei keinem andern Volk findet man den Adel, diesen ersten aller Stände, diese Grundlage jeder ständischen Verfassung, dieses erste und wesentlichste Naturelement des wahren Staats, mit so großen und starken Zügen gezeichnet, und in so reinen Verhältnissen, wie bei den Germanen . . . In dieser Hinsicht kann man sagen, die deutsche Geschichte, von der ältesten bis auf die neuesten Zeiten, sei eine natürliche und höchst lehrreiche Theorie des wahren Staats, d.h. der ständischen Verfassung." (*KA,* VII, 155 = *Bohn A,* p. 31.) All quotations from Bohn's Standard Library were compared with the original German and emended whenever necessary.
8. *KA,* VII, 208 = *Bohn A,* p. 88f.
9. *KA,* VII, 215 = *Bohn A,* p. 97.
10. *KA,* VII, 261 = *Bohn A,* pp. 147f.
11. *KA,* VII, 300 = *Bohn A,* pp. 191f.
12. *KA,* VI, 15 = *Bohn B,* p. 8.
13. *KA,* VI, 59 = *Bohn B,* p. 51.
14. "Die Nachahmung einer andern Nation führt nie zum Ziel, denn alles was diese in der Epoche ihrer vollendeten Entwicklung und auf der Höhe der Kunst hervorbringt, muß immer der nachbildenden fremd bleiben. Eine jede Nation darf aber nur zurückgehen auf ihre eigene ursprüngliche und älteste Poesie und Sage. Je näher die Quelle, je tiefer daraus geschöpft wird, je mehr tritt dasjenige hervor, was allen Nationen gemeinsam ist. Die Poesie der Nationen, so wie diese selbst, berührt sich in ihrem Ursprung." (*KA,* VI, 333 = *Bohn B,* p. 313.) It is characteristic of the different emphasis of the two versions of Schlegel's *Geschichte der alten und neuen Literatur* that the version of 1822 has the following two sentences added to the passage just quoted: "Der reine Born der religiösen Begeisterung aber bildet für alle Gemüter eine nie versiegende Quelle, aus deren Tiefe die Poesie immer wieder neu hervorgeht, und die jeder Zeit gleich nahe steht. Aus dieser Quelle schöpfte Lamartine seine Dichtungen, in denen der glückliche Anfang einer neuen Poesie für Frankreich aufgeht."

15. *KA*, VI, 237 = *Bohn B*, p. 225.
16. *KA*, VI, 197 = *Bohn B*, p. 187. My italics.
17. *KA*, VI, 213 = *Bohn B*, pp. 200f.
18. *KA*, VI, 281ff. = *Bohn B*, pp. 265ff.
19. "Es [das Wesen des Romantischen] beruht allein auf dem mit dem Christentum und durch dasselbe auch in der Poesie herrschenden Liebesgefühl, in welchem selbst das Leiden nur als Mittel der Verklärung erscheint, der tragische Ernst der alten Götterlehre und heidnischen Vorzeit in ein heiteres Spiel der Fantasie sich auflöst, und dann auch unter den äußern Formen der Darstellung und der Sprache solche gewählt werden, welche jenem inneren Liebesgefühl und Spiel der Fantasie entsprechen. In diesem Sinne, da das Romantische bloß die eigentümlich christliche Schönheit und Poesie bezeichnet, sollte wohl alle Poesie romantisch sein. In der Tat streitet auch das Romantische an sich mit dem Alten und wahrhaft Antiken nicht. Die Sage von Troja und die Homerischen Gesänge sind durchaus romantisch; so auch alles, was in indischen, persischen und andern alten orientalischen oder europäischen Gedichten wahrhaft poetisch ist. Wo irgend das höchste Leben mit Gefühl und ahndungsvoller Begeisterung in seiner tieferen Bedeutung ergriffen und dargestellt ist, da regen sich einzelne Anklänge wenigstens jener göttlichen Liebe, deren Mittelpunkt und volle Harmonie wir freilich erst im Christentum finden. Auch in den Tragikern der Alten sind die Anklänge dieses Gefühls ausgestreut und verbreitet, ungeachtet ihrer im ganzen finstern und dunkeln Weltansicht; die innere Liebe bricht in edeln Gemütern auch unter Irrtum und falschen Schreckbildern überall hervor. Nicht bloß die Kunst ist groß und bewundernswert im Äschylus und Sophokles, sondern auch die Gesinnung und das Gemüt. Nicht also in den lebendigen, nur in den künstlich gelehrten Dichtern des Altertums wird dieses liebevoll Romantische vermißt. Nicht dem Alten und Antiken, sondern nur dem unter uns fälschlich wieder aufgestellten Antikischen, allem was ohne innere Liebe bloß die Form der Alten nachkünstelt, ist das Romantische entgegengesetzt; so wie auf der andern Seite dem Modernen, d.h. demjenigen, was die Wirkung auf das Leben fälschlich dadurch zu erreichen sucht, daß es sich ganz an die Gegenwart anschließt, und in die Wirklichkeit einengt, wodurch es denn, wie sehr auch die Absicht und der Stoff verfeinert werden mag, der Herrschaft der beschränkten Zeit und Mode unvermeidlich anheim fällt." (*KA*, VI, 285f.; version of 1812. *Bohn B*, pp. 268f. provides a very inaccurate rendering of the version of 1822.) In fairness to Schlegel, it should be added that his conclusion loses some of its paradoxy in the light of the degeneration theory of religion. As he put it in his *Philosophie der Sprache* (1828): "If it is allowable, on

the ground that the true religion must from the very first have been one and the same, to give the name of Christianity to the simple religion of the first men and great saints of the primeval world, then we may well venture to assert that a vein of Christianity and of the knowledge of the true God runs through and ever and anon manifests itself through heathenism and its diverse mysteries." (*SW*, XV, 225 = *Bohn C*, p. 532.)

20. Cf. Polheim (1961).
21. Wellek and Warren, *Theory of Literature* (New York [1949]), p. 281.
22. *Deutsches Museum*, IV, 541 (Dec., 1813).
23. Cf. Behler (1966), p. 118.
24. *Walzel, Briefe*, pp. 545f.
25. *KA*, VII, xciv.
26. *Walzel, Briefe*, pp. 545f.
27. *KA*, VII, 408–27.
28. Cf. Ernst Behler in *KA*, VII, xciiiff.
29. Cf. *Krisenjahre*, III, 258, 473f.
30. *Walzel, Briefe*, p. 575.
31. Bleyer, pp. 105f.

Chapter Seven

1. *Finke*, p. 214.
2. *Krisenjahre*, II, 249.
3. His basic salary was 3000 *fl.* per annum; the rent for an apartment of 6–7 rooms in Vienna was approximately 5000 *fl.* in 1816. See J. K. Mayr, *Geschichte der österreichischen Staatskanzlei im Zeitalter des Fürsten Metternich* (Vienna, 1935), pp. 115ff.
4. *Krisenjahre*, I, 127.
5. Jean de Pange, A.-G. *Schlegel et Madame de Staël, d'après des documents inédits* (Paris, 1938), pp. 129ff.
6. *Unger*, p. 49.
7. *Krisenjahre*, I, 345.
8. *Ibid.*, II, 100.
9. *Ibid.*, II, 144.
10. *Ibid.*, II, 195.
11. *Ibid.*, II, 213.
12. Cf., e.g., *Allgemeines Litteratur-Archiv*, XV, 437f., 441; *Krisenjahre*, II, 364; *Walzel, Briefe*, pp. 540, 644, 648; *Rottmanner*, I, 58, 175, 184, 196.
13. Detlev W. Schumann, "Konvertitenbriefe," *Literaturwissenschaftliches Jahrbuch der Görres-Gesellschaft*, N.F. III (1962), p. 91.
14. Benjamin Constant, *Journal intime*, October, 1804.

15. Quoted from Eichler, pp. 272f.

16. *Briefe von Gentz an Pilat,* ed. K. Mendelssohn-Bartholdy (Leipzig, 1868), I, 314f.

17. *Aus dem Nachlaß Varnhagens von Ense. Briefwechsel . . .* (Leipzig, 1874–75), VI, 136.

18. Cf. *Rottmanner,* I, xviiiff. and Anstett, pp. 318–32.

19. *Ibid.,* p. 35.

20. For a more detailed account, see Behler (1967).

21. *Concordia,* pp. 1 and 2; my italics. Cf. Behler (1967), p. 25.

22. *Concordia,* i, 3–70; iii, 164–90; vi, 343–98. Reprinted in *KA,* VII, 483–596.

23. *KA,* VII, 492.

24. *Ibid.,* pp. 489, 493f.

25. *Ibid.,* pp. 496, 500; "English sickness" was a common expression for syphilis.

26. *Ibid.,* p. 513.

27. *Ibid.,* p. 538.

28. *Ibid.,* pp. 546, 554, 584.

29. *Ibid.,* pp. 543f., 585.

30. *Ibid.,* pp. 490f.

31. *Ibid.,* p. 527.

32. *Briefwechsel zwischen F. Gentz und A. H. Müller* (Stuttgart, 1857), p. 330.

33. Cf. p. 137 below.

34. *Körner, F. u. D.,* p. 254.

35. Schlegel considered the numbers 7 and 33 to have mystical significance. Prophecies that 1836 was to be the year of the Judgment had been widespread in Germany for some time. In the "Signatur des Zeitalters," Schlegel had called these prophecies "false, or at least very arbitrary and absolutely unjustified" (*KA,* VII, 502).

36. *Rottmanner,* II, 7, 89, 145.

37. *Ibid.,* II, 89.

38. *Körner, F. u. D.,* p. 9.

39. *KA,* XVIII, 216 [262]; cf. 317 [1501]. Subsequently, Schlegel's conviction of the inadequacy of discursive reasoning in theological matters was greatly strengthened by his study of Böhme.

40. *SW,* XV, 20f. = *Bohn C,* p. 362.

41. *SW,* XV, 92 = *Bohn C,* p. 92.

42. Cf., e.g., *SW,* XII, 72. There is an ironic touch in the fact that Fichte, all appearances to the contrary, was no less eager than Schlegel to claim that *his* philosophy was an empirical science. Thus, for example, he specified in 1801 that the "innermost spirit and soul" of his system was the assertion that "man has absolutely nothing whatever but experience, and attains everything he does attain exclusively

through experience." (Fichte's *Sämtliche Werke*, ed. J. H. Fichte [Berlin, 1845ff.], II, 333f.)

43. *SW*, XII, 17 = *Bohn C*, pp. 11f.

44. *SW*, XII, 213; cf. *KA*, VI, 213.

45. *SW*, XII, 71ff. To trace the workings of divine providence was the main purpose of Schlegel's *Philosophie der Geschichte;* but as the interpretation of the course of history offered in this work is based on Christian convictions, the argument is circular.

46. *SW*, XII, 26f. Among Schlegel's contemporaries, C. T. H. Windischmann and J. Molitor proposed a similar trichotomy, but the principle is, of course, very much older. Cf., e.g., Plotinus' distinction of *nous, psyche,* and *physis,* and I. Thessalonians 5, v. 23: "And I pray God your whole spirit and soul and body be preserved blameless unto the coming of the Lord Jesus Christ."

47. *SW*, XII, 293ff.; XV, 119, 142, 145f., 179f.; *KA*, II, 356ff.

48. *SW*, XIII, 132f. = *Bohn D*, p. 163.

49. *SW*, XIII, 131–45; XV, 122.

50. *KA*, VI, 399. Cf. Behler (1966), pp. 143f.

51. See Behler (1963a).

52. *Rottmanner*, II, 233.

53. *Ibid.*

54. *Ibid.*, II, 297f.

55. *SW*, XIII, 115 = *Bohn D*, p. 149.

56. *SW*, XIII, 44 = *Bohn D*, p. 91. Cf. *SW*, XV, 59ff. What Schlegel meant by "the internal word" is explained in the *Philosophie des Lebens,* where he surmises that man originally had the "power of communicating his thoughts to others inwardly, through the will alone, without the external means of language." (*SW*, XII, 299.)

57. *SW*, XIII, 172ff. = *Bohn D*, pp. 193ff.

58. *SW*, XIII, 37 = *Bohn D*, p. 85.

59. *SW*, XII, 92, 268ff.; XIII, 59ff. = *Bohn C*, pp. 80, 241; *D*, p. 59.

60. Cf. Behler (1960), pp. 341f.

61. They will be reprinted in *KA*, IX–X.

62. *SW*, XV, 253; omitted in *Bohn D*.

63. Cf. Tieck's report in *Findlinge zur Geschichte der alten Sprache und Dichtung,* ed. H. v. Fallersleben, I (Leipzig, 1860), 150.

64. *Das Inland.* Ein Tagblatt für das öffentliche Leben in Deutschland . . . 1829, Nr. 31 (Feb. 10), p. 123. Cf. Karl Gutzkow's preface to the second edition of Schleiermacher's *Vertraute Briefe über F. Schlegels Lucinde* (Hamburg, 1835), p. xxxv.

65. Wellek, II, 35.

Selected Bibliography

In sections A, B, and C of the Bibliography, every entry is preceded, in the left-hand margin, by the abbreviation used to refer to it in the Notes.

PRIMARY SOURCES

A. Works by Friedrich Schlegel

KA = *Kritische Friedrich-Schlegel-Ausgabe.* Ed. Ernst Behler in collaboration with Jean-Jacques Anstett and Hans Eichner. Munich-Paderborn-Vienna: Ferdinand Schöningh, Zurich: Thomas-Verlag, 1957ff.

So far, the following volumes have appeared:

Vol. II: *Charakteristiken und Kritiken I (1796–1801).* Ed. Hans Eichner, 1966.

Vol. IV: *Ansichten und Ideen von der christlichen Kunst.* Ed. Hans Eichner, 1959.

Vol. V: *Dichtungen.* Ed. Hans Eichner, 1962.

Vol. VI: *Geschichte der alten und neuen Literatur.* Ed. Hans Eichner, 1961.

Vol. VII: *Studien zur Geschichte und Politik.* Ed. Ernst Behler, 1966.

Vol. X: *Philosophie des Lebens. Philosophie der Sprache und des Wortes.* Ed. Ernst Behler, 1969. (Published too late to be used in the present volume.)

Vol. XI: *Wissenschaft der europäischen Literatur.* Ed. Ernst Behler, 1958.

Vols. XII and XIII: *Philosophische Vorlesungen (1800–1807).* Ed. J.-J. Anstett, 1964.

Vol. XIV: *Vorlesungen über Universalgeschichte (1805–1806).* Ed. J.-J. Anstett, 1960.

Vol. XVIII: *Philosophische Lehrjahre (1796–1806). I.* Ed. Ernst Behler, 1963.

As the critical edition is making rapid progress, it would serve little purpose to provide an extensive bibliography of Schlegel's writings. The following texts are quoted frequently in the present work:

DNL 143 = August Wilhelm und Friedrich Schlegel. Selections by Oskar F. Walzel. Stuttgart: Deutsche Verlagsgesellschaft, n.d. (= Deutsche National-Litteratur, vol. 143).

Indier = F. Schlegel. Von der Sprache und Weisheit der Indier. Heidelberg: Mohr und Zimmer, 1808.

Lessing = Lessings Gedanken und Meinungen aus dessen Schriften, compiled and annotated by Friedrich Schlegel. Leipzig: Juniussische Buchhandlung, 1804. 3 vols.

LN = F. Schlegel. Literary Notebooks 1797–1801, edited with introduction and commentary by Hans Eichner. London: Athlone Press, 1957.

Minor = Friedrich Schlegel, 1794–1802: Seine prosaischen Jugendschriften. Ed. J. Minor. Wien: Carl Konegen, 1882. 2 vols.

N.ph.Sch. = F. Schlegel, *Neue philosophische Schriften.* Ed. Josef Körner. Frankfurt a.M.: G. Schulte-Bulmke, 1935.

SW = Friedrich von Schlegels sämtliche Werke. Zweite Original-Ausgabe. Vienna: Ignaz Klang, 1846. 15 vols.

B. Letters

Boisserée = Sulpiz Boisserée. Ed. Mathilde Boisserée. Stuttgart: Cotta, 1862. 2 vols.

Caroline = Caroline, Briefe aus der Frühromantik. Ed. Erich Schmidt. Leipzig: Insel-Verlag, 1913. 2 vols.

Dorothea = Dorothea v. Schlegel geb. Mendelssohn und deren Söhne Joh. u. Ph. Veit, Briefwechsel . . . Ed. J. M. Raich. Mainz: Franz Kirchheim, 1881. 2 vols.

Finke = Der Briefwechsel F. u. D. Schlegels 1818–1820. Ed. Heinrich Finke. München: Kösel & Pustet, 1923.

Jonas-Dilthey = Aus Schleiermachers Leben: In Briefen. Ed. Ludwig Jonas and Wilhelm Dilthey. Berlin: Georg Reimer, 1858–1863. 4 vols.

Körner, F. u. D. = Briefe von und an F. u . D. Schlegel. Ed. Josef Körner. Berlin: Askanischer Verlag, 1926.

Krisenjahre = Krisenjahre der Frühromantik. Briefe aus dem Schlegelkreis, Ed. Josef Körner. Brünn-Vienna-Leipzig: Rudolf M. Rohrer, 1936–37 (vols. I and II); Bern: A. Francke, 1958 (vol. III).

Preitz = F. Schlegel und Novalis: Biographie einer Romantikerfreundschaft in ihren Briefen . . . Ed. Max Preitz. Darmstadt: Gentner, 1957.

Rottmanner = Schlegels Briefe an Frau Christine Stransky . . . Ed. M. Rottmanner. Wien: Verlag des Literarischen Vereins, 1907 and 1916. (= Schriften des Literarischen Vereins in Wien, vols. VII and XVI.)

Unger = Briefe von D. u. F. Schlegel an die Familie Paulus, Ed.

Rudolf Unger. Berlin: B. Behr, 1913. (= Deutsche Literatur-denkmale des 18. und 19. Jahrhunderts, vol. 146.)

Walzel, Briefe = *Schlegels Briefe an seinen Bruder August Wilhelm,* Ed. Oskar F. Walzel. Berlin: Speyer & Peters, 1890.

C. Translations

Bohn A = Frederick Schlegel. *A Course of Lectures on Modern History* . . . tr. by Lyndsey Purcell and R. H. Whitelock. London: H. G. Bohn, 1849.

Bohn B = Frederick Schlegel. *Lectures on the History of Literature, Ancient and Modern* . . . [tr. by H. G. Bohn *et al.*] London: H. G. Bohn, 1859.

Bohn C = Frederick Schlegel. *The Philosophy of Life and Philosophy of Language* . . . tr. by A. J. W. Morrison. London: H. G. Bohn, 1847.

Bohn D = Frederick Schlegel. *The Philosophy of History* . . . tr. from the German, with a memoir of the author, by J. B. Robertson. The revised ed. London: H. G. Bohn, 1859.

Bohn E = *The Aesthetic and Miscellaneous Works of Frederick von Schlegel,* comprising Letters on Christian Art/Essay on Gothic Architecture/Remarks on the Romance-Poetry of the Middle Ages and on Shakespeare/On the Limits of the Beautiful/On the Language and Wisdom of the Indians. Tr. by E. J. Millington. London: H. G. Bohn, 1860.

(The translations of Schlegel's essays on art in the last-named volume are based on the revised versions of 1822–25. The only English translation of *Lucinde* [*The German Classics.* Masterpieces of German Literature translated into English. Vol. IV. New York, 1913, pp. 124–74] is abridged to about half the original length, and thus totally useless. With the exception of a few short extracts, none of the rest of Schlegel's early writings is available in English; there is, however, an excellent French translation of Schlegel's novel: *Lucinde,* roman; introduction, traduction et notes de J.-J. Anstett, [Paris, 1943].)

Since the completion of the present book, an excellent volume of translations has appeared: Friedrich Schlegel, *Dialogue on Poetry and Literary Aphorisms.* Translated, introduced, and annotated by Ernst Behler and Roman Struc. University Park and London: The Pennsylvania State University Press, 1968.

D. Periodicals Edited by Schlegel

Athenäum. Eine Zeitschrift von A. W. Schlegel u. F. Schlegel. Berlin: Friedrich Vieweg, 1798. Heinrich Frölich, 1799–1800.

Europa. Eine Zeitschrift, Ed. F. Schlegel. Frankfurt a.M.: Friedrich
Wilmans, 1803–1805.

Deutsches Museum, Ed. F. Schlegel. Wien: Camesinasche Buchhandlung, 1812–13.

Concordia, Eine Zeitschrift, Ed. F. Schlegel. Wien: J. B. Wallishausser,
1820–23.

(The *Athenäum, Europa,* and *Concordia* are easily accessible in the
form of photomechanical reprints; for details, see the next section of the
Bibliography under Behler. A similar reprint of the *Deutsches Museum*
is in preparation.)

SECONDARY SOURCES

ALLEMANN, BEDA. *Ironie und Dichtung: F. Schlegel, Novalis, Solger,
Kierkegaard, Nietzsche, Thomas Mann, Musil.* Pfullingen: Neske,
1956; 2nd ed., 1969. A stimulating discussion of the concepts of
irony entertained by the authors named in the title.

ANSTETT, JEAN-JACQUES. *La pensée religieuse de F. Schlegel.* Paris:
Société d'Edition Les Belles Lettres, 1941. The standard work
on Schlegel's religious thought.

BAUSCH, WALTER. *Theorien des epischen Erzählens in der deutschen
Frühromantik.* Bonn: H. Bouvier & Co., 1964. (Bonner Arbeiten
zur deutschen Literatur, vol. VIII.) A better-than-average doctoral dissertation, dealing far more extensively with F. Schlegel's
theories of narrative fiction than with those of the other early
Romantics.

BEHLER, ERNST. "F. Schlegels Theorie der Universalpoesie," *Jahrbuch
der Deutschen Schillergesellschaft,* I (1957), 211–52.

——. "F. Schlegel im Portrait," *Zeitschrift für Kunstwissenschaft,*
XIII (1959), 91–110.

——. "Zur Theologie der Romantik: Das Gottesproblem in der
Spätphilosophie F. Schlegels," *Hochland,* LII (1960), 339–53.

——. "*Athenäum:* Die Geschichte einer Zeitschrift." (Postscript to
the photomechanical reprint of the *Athenäum* [Stuttgart: Wissenschaftliche Buchgesellschaft, 1960].)

——. "F. Schlegel und Hegel," *Hegel-Studien,* I (1963), 203–50.
(Quoted as Behler [1963a].)

——. "*Europa:* Die Geschichte einer Zeitschrift." (Postscript to the
photomechanical reprint of *Europa* [Darmstadt: Wissenschaftliche
Buchgesellschaft, 1963]; quoted as Behler [1963b].)

——. "F. Schlegel in Selbstzeugnissen und Bilddokumenten. Rein-
bek: Rowohlt, 1966. A brilliantly written, short account of Schlegel's life and works by a leading expert.

————. *"Concordia:* Die Geschichte einer Zeitschrift." (Postscript to the photomechanical reprint of *Concordia* [Darmstadt: Wissenschaftliche Buchgesellschaft, 1967].)

BLEYER, JAKOB. *F. Schlegel am Bundestage in Frankfurt.* Ungedruckte Briefe . . . nebst amtlichen Berichten und Denkschriften aus den Jahren 1815–1818. München-Leipzig: Duncker & Humblot, 1913. A profusely documented account of Schlegel's activities in Frankfurt.

BORCHERDT, HANS HEINRICH. *Schiller und die Romantik. Briefe und Dokumente.* Stuttgart: Cotta [1948]. A convenient compilation of letters and documents; the editor's comments are occasionally unreliable.

BRINKMANN, RICHARD. "Romantische Dichtungstheorie in F. Schlegels Frühschriften und Schillers Begriffe des Naiven und Sentimentalischen," *Deutsche Vierteljahrsschrift,* XXXII (1958), 344–71.

DIECKMANN, LISELOTTE. "The Metaphor of Hieroglyphics in German Romanticism," *Comparative Literature,* VII (1955), 306–12.

————. "F. Schlegel and Romantic Concepts of the Symbol," *Germanic Review,* XXIV (1959), 276–83.

DILTHEY, WILHELM. *Leben Schleiermachers.* Vol. I, Berlin: Georg Reimer, 1870. (No further volumes published.) This brilliant study of the first half of Schleiermacher's life contains detailed and perspicacious discussions of F. Schlegel's personality and intellectual development; its importance is not substantially diminished by Dilthey's evident bias against Schlegel.

EICHLER, HERBERT. "F. Schlegel 1808–1815." (University of Vienna doctoral dissertation, 1927. Typescript.) This scholarly and painstaking unpublished dissertation still contains valuable information not to be found elsewhere.

EICHNER, HANS. "The Supposed Influence of Schiller's *Über naive und sentimentale Dichtung* on F. Schlegel's *Über das Studium der griechischen Poesie,*" *Germanic Review,* XXX (1955), 260–64.

————. "F. Schlegel's Theory of Romantic Poetry," *PMLA,* LXXI (1956), 1018–41.

————. "Neues aus F. Schlegels Nachlaß," *Jahrbuch der Deutschen Schillergesellschaft,* III (1959), 218–43.

ENDERS, CARL. *F. Schlegel: Die Quellen seines Wesens und Werdens.* Leipzig: H. Haessel, 1913. This detailed study of Schlegel's youth —up to 1799— is still valuable, but has been made obsolete in some respects by later research.

ENGEL-JÁNOSI, FRIEDRICH. "Die Theorie vom Staat im deutschen Österreich 1815–1848," *Zeitschrift für öffentliches Recht,* II (1921), 360–94.

GÉRARD, RENÉ. *L'Orient et la pensée romantique allemande*. Paris: Marcel Didier, 1963. A scholarly treatment of an important aspect of German Romanticism.

GUNDOLF, FRIEDRICH. "F. Schlegels romantische Schriften," *Jahrbuch des Freien Deutschen Hochstifts*, 1927, pp. 28–120. (Reprinted in Gundolf's collection of essays, *Romantiker* [Berlin: H. Keller, 1930].)

HATFIELD, HENRY. "*Wilhelm Meisters Lehrjahre* and 'Progressive Universalpoesie'," *Germanic Review*, XXXVI (1961), 221–29.

HAYM, RUDOLF. *Die romantische Schule*. Berlin: Rudolf Gaertner, 1870. Almost a century later, and in spite of Haym's obvious prejudices against certain aspects of German Romanticism, this monumental study of the early stages of the movement is still unsurpassed in the depth and brilliance of its exposition.

HENDRIX, J. P. *Das politische Weltbild F. Schlegels*. Bonn: H. Bouvier, 1962. (= Schriften zur Rechtslehre und Politik, vol. XXXVI.) A competent presentation of Schlegel's political views.

IMMERWAHR, RAYMOND. "The Subjectivity or Objectivity of F. Schlegel's Poetic Irony," *Germanic Review*, XXVI (1951), 173–90.

———. "Germanic Romanticism and the Unity of the Romantic Imagination," in: *On Romanticism and the Art of Translation: Studies in Honor of E. H. Zeydel*, ed. G. F. Merkel. Princeton, 1956.

———. "F. Schlegel's Essay 'On Goethe's *Meister*'," *Monatshefte*, XLIX (1957), 1–21.

———. "The First Romantic Aesthetics," *Modern Language Quarterly*, XXXI (1960), 3–26. Analysis of late eighteenth-century treatises on gardening and landscaping and their bearing on literary developments.

KLUCKHOHN, PAUL. *Die Auffassung der Liebe im 18. Jahrhundert und in der Romantik*. 2nd ed. Halle: Niemeyer, 1931. The 1966 reprint of this important study has an index.

KÖRNER, JOSEF. *Romantiker und Klassiker: Die Brüder Schlegel in ihren Beziehungen zu Schiller und Goethe*. Berlin: Askanischer Verlag, 1924. This detailed account of the relations of Goethe and Schiller with the brothers Schlegel is partly based on materials still unpublished.

———. "Das Problem Friedrich Schlegel," *Germanisch-Romanische Monatsschrift*, XVI (1928), 274–97.

———. "F. Schlegels philosophische Lehrjahre," in F. Schlegel, *Neue philosophische Schriften* (Frankfurt a.M., 1935), pp. 3–114. (Quoted as *N.ph.Sch.*)

KRÜGER, JOHANNA. "F. Schlegels Bekehrung zu Lessing." Weimar: Alexander Duncker, 1913. (= Forschungen zur neueren Literaturgeschichte, vol. XLV.) The emphasis of this excellent study rests mainly on Schlegel's attitude to Lessing during the 1790's.

LANGE, VICTOR. "F. Schlegel's Literary Criticism," *Comparative Literature*, VII (1955), 289–305.

LEMPICKI, SIGMUND VON. "Bücherwelt und wirkliche Welt: Ein Beitrag zur Wesenserfassung der Romantik," *Deutsche Vierteljahrsschrift*, III (1925), 339–86.

LORENZ, REINHOLD. "F. Schlegels Wiener Vorlesungen über die Neuere Geschichte," *Deutsche Vierteljahrsschrift*, IV (1926), 696–717.

LOVEJOY, A. O. *Essays in the History of Ideas*. New York: G. Braziller, 1955. The articles on Schlegel in this volume—"The Meaning of 'Romantic' in Early German Romanticism" and "Schiller and the Genesis of Romanticism"—date from 1916/17 and 1920, respectively; important when first published, they have been largely superseded by more recent research and the discovery of new source materials.

MARTIN, ALFRED. "Romantischer 'Katholizismus' und katholische 'Romantik'," *Hochland*, XXIII (1926), pp. 315ff.

————. "Romantische Konversionen," *Logos*, XVII (1928), 141–64.

MAUTNER, FRANZ H. "Der Aphorismus als literarische Gattung," *Zeitschrift für Aesthetik*, XXVII (1933), 132–75.

METTLER, WERNER. *Der junge F. Schlegel und die griechische Literatur: Ein Beitrag zum Problem der Historie*. Zurich: Atlantis Verlag, 1955. (= Züricher Beiträge zur deutschen Literatur- und Geistesgeschichte, vol. XI.) An analysis of Schlegel's *Geschichte der Poesie der Griechen und Römer*, emphasizing its significance for the development of literary historiography; useful and stimulating, though insufficient attention to other late eighteenth-century histories of literature has resulted in some oversimplifications.

MÜLLER, GÜNTHER. "Einführung," in: F. Schlegel, *Von der Seele*. Augsburg-Köln: Benno Filser, 1927.

MÜLLER, KARL. *F. Schlegels Konversion im Zusammenhang seiner weltanschaulichen Entwicklung*. Gießen: Nitschkowski, 1928. One of the better doctoral dissertations on Schlegel.

NEWE, HEINRICH. "Die Philosophie F. Schlegels in den Jahren 1804–1806," *Philosophisches Jahrbuch der Görres-Gesellschaft*, XLIII (1930), 373–87, 499–509.

OPPENBERG, URSULA. *Quellenstudien zu F. Schlegels Übersetzungen aus dem Sanskrit*. Marburg: N. G. Elwert, 1965 (= Marburger Beiträge zur Germanistik, vol. VII). A critical examination of Schlegel's translations from Sanskrit, his sources, and his competence as a Sanskrit scholar.

PAULSEN, WOLFGANG. "F. Schlegels *Lucinde* als Roman," *Germanic Review*, XXI (1946), 173ff.

POLHEIM, K. K. "Spätzeiten als Frühzeiten," *Wirkendes Wort*, XI

(1961), 74–82. Contains an analysis of the ways in which Schlegel's theory of the novel anticipates twentieth-century developments.

————. "Nachwort," in F. Schlegel, *Lucinde*. Stuttgart: Reclams Universal-Bibliothek, 1963.

————. *Die Arabeske: Ansichten und Ideen aus F. Schlegels Poetik*. Munich-Paderborn-Vienna: Schoeningh, 1966. This thorough examination of one of Schlegel's key concepts, the arabesque, sheds light on the whole of Schlegel's literary criticism. Though not easy to read, this is the best of the many studies of Schlegel's poetics.

ROBSON–SCOTT, W. D. *The Literary Background of the Gothic Revival in Germany: A* Chapter in the History of Taste. Oxford: Clarendon Press, 1965. This excellent study provides a short, but definitive assessment of Schlegel's contribution to the Gothic Revival.

ROUGE, J. *F. Schlegel et la genèse du romantisme allemand, 1791–97*. (= Bibliothèque des Universités du Midi, Fasc. VIII.) Paris: A. Fontemoing and Bordeaux: Feret & Fils, 1904. An interesting presentation of Schlegel's beginnings.

————. "Le culte du 'moi' et la culture du 'moi' chez F. Schlegel," *Revue de métaphysique et de morale*, XLI (1934), 205–31.

RÜHLE-GERSTEL, A. "F. Schlegel und Chamfort," *Euphorion*, XXIV (1922), 809–60.

SCHLAGDENHAUFFEN, ALFRED. *Frédéric Schlegel et son groupe: La doctrine de l' "Athenaeum"* (1798–1800). Paris: Belles Lettres, 1934. (= Publications de la Faculté des lettres de l'Université de Strasbourg, Fasc. 64.) A comprehensive and mature study of the *Athenäum*.

SCHLEIERMACHER, FRIEDRICH. *Vertraute Briefe über F. Schlegels Lucinde*. Lübeck-Leipzig, 1800. Schleiermacher's defense of Schlegel's novel—published anonymously—is still of considerable interest.

SCHUMANN, G. M. "F. Schlegels Umarbeitung seiner Schriften für die Gesamtausgabe." (University of Munich doctoral dissertation, 1911.) A study of the revisions Schlegel made in preparing his writings for the *Collected Works* of 1822–25.

SIEMES, J. B. "F. Schlegel als Vorläufer christlicher Existenzphilosophie," *Scholastik*, XXX (1955), 161–84.

SPANN, MENO. "Progressive Universalpoesie," *Monatshefte*, XXVIII (1930), 1–7.

STROHSCHNEIDER-KOHRS, INGRID. *Die romantische Ironie in Theorie und Gestaltung*. Tübingen: Niemeyer, 1960. (= Hermaea. Germanistische Forschungen. Neue Folge, vol. VI.) A thorough and perceptive study of the concepts and uses of irony in German

Romanticism, which suffers, however, from the author's failure to place the subject in its proper historical perspective.

SZONDI, PETER. "F. Schlegel und die romantische Ironie," *Euphorion,* XLVIII (1954), 397–411.

TWADDELL, W. F. "F. Schlegel's Criteria of Linguistic Relations," *Monatshefte,* XXXV (1943), 151–55.

ULLMANN, L. and H. GOTTHARD. *Geschichte des Begriffes "Romantisch" in Deutschland . . . bis ins dritte Jahrzehnt des 19. Jahrhunderts.* Germanistische Studien, vol. 50. Berlin, 1927. Though not always very profound in its analyses, this monograph is a monument of industry and indispensable to any serious study of the subject.

WALZEL, OSKAR F. *Romantisches.* Bonn: Röhrscheid, 1934. (= Mnemosyne, vol. XVIII.) A large portion of this book by a famous scholar deals with F. Schlegel's esthetics.

———. "F. Schlegels 'Gespräch über die Poesie'," *Poesie und Nichtpoesie.* Frankfurt a.M.: Schulte-Bulmke, 1937, pp. 112–47.

WELLEK, RENÉ. "Friedrich Schlegel," *A History of Modern Criticism.* New Haven: Yale University Press, 1955f., II, 5–35.

WIESE, BENNO VON. *F. Schlegel: Ein Beitrag zur Geschichte der romantischen Konversionen.* Philosophische Forschungen, vol. VI. Berlin: Springer, 1927.

WILLSON, A. L. *A Mythical Image: The Ideal of India in German Romanticism.* Durham, N, C.: Duke University Press, 1964. This study and the one by Gérard listed above in many ways supplement each other.

Index